A PRIVATE DEVOTIONAL DIARY

A Private Devotional Diary

Edited by John Birkbeck

JOHN KNOX PRESS
ATLANTA

Library of Congress Cataloging in Publication Data
Main entry under title:

A Private devotional diary.

    Includes index.
    1. Devotional calendars. I. Birkbeck, John,
1908-
BV4810.P64   242'.2   75-13465
ISBN 0-8042-2511-7

To the glory of God
and
in gratitude to Him for
John Wright Stevenson
(1903-1973)
Anmchara (Soul friend)*
Spiritual director to many

* Early Celtic Church title

PREFACE

Scotland has long been regarded as a fount of theology, but few associate the Kirk with devotional literature. Yet, there is a wealth of material available illustrative of the preaching and teaching that has nourished the piety and Christian practice of the Scot from the earliest days.

Mr. Birkbeck has had the imagination, the energy, and the catholicity of taste to assemble a remarkable collection of extracts from representatives of this tradition. They span the centuries from the Celtic Church to the present day and are drawn from the works of men and women of all kinds of churchmanship.

This is a book to browse in to meet old friends and to make new ones. Many will find themselves impelled to follow up a new acquaintance by tracking down the book from which the extract is made. All will benefit from the exposure to such a wide range of Christian devotion and delight in the insights of those who shared their love of Christ through the pulpit or printed page.

It has been said that the Scottish contribution to the Church Universal has been a combination of "scholarship and passion." Something of this can be gleaned from these pages. The book will be welcomed as a happy companion to such a classic as John Baillie's *Dairy of Private Prayer*.

David H. C. Read
Madison Avenue Presbyterian Church
New York City

INTRODUCTION

On his celebrated journey through the Western Isles, Dr. Samuel Johnson expressed astonishment in finding men "who lived in huts and quoted Latin." This did not deter him taunting James Boswell, "Can you name one book of any value on a religious subject written by the Scottish clergy?" History is tantalisingly silent on whether or not this distinguished man of letters was ever enlightened.

By what has been written and also not written, it is evident that many within the bounds of Scotland and furth of it are oblivious to the fascinating heritage of the nation which touches life at its deepest and which reveals an appealing grandeur of style. No one who has taken care to find out will gainsay that the contribution of Scotland to the religious literature of the world has positive distinction.

This diary is no attempt to quarry the whole field of this heritage. It is an outline to awaken the mind, to sustain the soul, to comfort and to challenge, to enthuse and to excite, to evidence the life which is in Christ.

Research makes plain that there is an embarrassment of riches in the selection of the devotional material available. A gracious blending of theology, scholarship, and a devotional spirit determined the canon of choice. The distillation of a gift with words, captured in print, was not ignored.

The dust of past and present controversy is not disturbed. No historical criticism, no overall judgment, no yearning after a romantic past, lent influence to the compiling. The sad mistakes and shames of other years are not glossed over. Time and grace have mellowed them into humbling and helpful lessons. The holiness of origin, the action of history, the responsibility and opportunity of the present, find clear utterance in these preferences. The undeniable spiritual truth made lucid and virile by men and women of diverse emphasis and elements of faith in Scotland's striving and achievement is objectively set forth.

The first thousand years present barely a figure of whom a constructive biography remains. Scarce any records and few contemporary narratives survived pillage and the eroding of time. Yet some authentic information is preserved to compensate for the welter of fable, legend, confusion, annotation, revisions, imagination, which cluttered documents penned over those years. How grateful Scotland ought to be to those historians who have sifted fact from fantasy and given access to the positives, the affirmations, the benefactions of a dark and necessitous Scotland.

Robert Burns counselled that there was virtue in seeing *"oursels as ithers see us."* For this reason it is worthy to note that a certain Ordericus Vitalis, a Norman monk of St. Evroul, speaking of the year 1068 A.D., writes in his *Historia Ecclesiastica,* "The Scottish nation, although fierce in battle, love ease and quiet, and has no desire for disturbance by neighbouring kingdoms, being bent on the study of the Christian faith rather than on the exercise of arms." Benevolent historians are not invited to comment!

This certainty stands inviolate in the long story of Scotland. In times of savagery and suffering when deep darkness prevailed, there was kept alive among devout souls some "sponk" of God's light. Men and women full of zeal and love of God, of prayer and true piety, utterly without assumption, who had seen some angle of God's radiant thought, discoursed of God and Destiny, of the Christ of human love and hope. These kindlers scattered the sacred fire of their passion as they moved among their time. For these well-known, scarce-known, unknown to fame who, with complete absence of exaggeration and free of all theorising wrote and lived the life in Christ, to God alone be the glory.

Looking at the rock from which Scotland's spiritual life was hewn, some facts are salient. In the early Celtic Church there is hardly a boundary felt between the Divine country and the earthly. The preaching was Biblical in character. Verbum Dei was the only criterion. The Church was evangelical in the healthiest and truest interpretation. Those old time ghillies of God, the Culdees, found the Bible no text-book listing lawful doctrines. It was the living word of the living Christ. With sincerity they taught the innate sinfulness of natural man, the reconciling death of Christ, justification by faith without the merit of works. The sacraments were signs and seals of the one grace through Christ, and as such held only second place in their teaching. It is not without significance that the last transcription of St. Columba was that sentence in Psalm 34—"They that seek the Lord shall want no manner of thing that is good."

The Scot has always had to wrestle hard to win a living from a reluctant nature. This habit influenced the pattern of his thinking. Proof is required for every claim. Argument must be followed to the extreme and compromise despised. Little wonder that Wilfred despaired after debate with Colman at the Council of Whitby in 664 A.D.—*"The only people stupid* enough to disagree with the whole world are these Scots and their obstinate adherents the Picts, who inhabit only a portion of these two islands in the remote ocean." The Scot has no delight in wandering mazes. His mind ever abhors vagueness and irresolution. Coveting intelligence and doctrine, he would have both wedded to life. The devotional writings corroborate these traits.

It is claimed by some that no Scottish devotional composition can hold a candle to *The Imitation of Christ,* prove as vivid as *The Pilgrim's Progress,* equal Jeremy Taylor in appeal and style, and compare with the beauty of the *English Prayer Book.* This could be true. But you cannot slay the immortal! The greatness of Scottish devotional literature reveals no primary pursuit after intellectualism, imagination, eloquence. Though these be highly essential, the stress has been the search after crystal clearness of thought, a sanctified common sense, a pithiness of phrase which seek to guide a serious soul to God.

Consider some of the evidence: John Knox's *Liturgy* which has enriched worship with utterances unrivalled. The *Letters* of Samuel Rutherford with their searching thoughts and deep spiritual affinity. Henry Scougal's *Life of God in the Soul of Man,* that mirror of a mind seeking beauty and purity. *The Sacramental Catechism* of John Willison in all its power and sensitivity. Robert Bruce and his cogent sermons. Fraser of Alness, a man of Ciceronian intellect, stressing the means of Sanctification. The *Letters* of Thomas Erskine of Linlathen, misty and mystical, yet bathed with the wonder of God's love.

The register of those who fed the life of prayer, of praise, of adoration; who summoned others to venture after high and abiding things; who communicated, to all Scotland and to the Church Universal, the meditative mind and baptised them with the passion of gratitude and sacrifice.... Why, the time fails to tell of men and women who would rather be "found in Christ" than "lost in God," and who hunted for truth as the blind long for light. Of such could be said, as was said of Robert Leighton, *"A purer, humbler, holier spirit never tabernacled in Scottish clay."*

They took men and women straight to the Bible—the fountain of all true piety. The Psalter was deemed the "devotional book of the world." The metrical version was designed as a ready aid to remembering the thought and language of the Psalter. With the paraphrasing of passages from the Old and the New Testaments came a greater and stronger foundation to Biblical narrative. In homes by night folk sang the Scriptures and by day meditated upon its truth and relevance. Despite the rugged rhymes and stately speech, it was the living Bible in the vernacular. The theologian was born in the Bible.

Preachers who quickened their mental faculties, broadened their sympathies, and who spoke with authority and conviction liberated their minds from the shackles of their age, and wrought an ennobling influence. They challenged the attention of the world. They rewarded the thoughtful. They preferred truth to ornament. They spoke to the aspiring life of their day. They proved that in faith was sound logic. In earnestness they pled from conviction and compulsion.

A minister from Kincardine-on-Forth got this letter from Thomas Chalmers: *"Mind the three P's. Aim at Proving, Painting, and Persuading."* In other words, address the Reason, the Fancy, and the Heart. So it was that, under the tuition of the Holy Spirit, the preachers in Scotland opened the sluices of gratitude in the driest heart.

This diary culled from a nation's faith and practice has its contribution won from every communion of the Church. Eternal, unchanging, truth belongs to God. He imparts illumination and inspiration through every church born of His will and kept by His power. These devotions come from Christians of all persuasions who confess: *"I believe in One Holy, Catholic and Apostolic Church."*

The men and women whose spiritual insight is included in these pages are all either Scots born or trained and ministered in Scotland. They all show much of Andrew Melville's courage and candour, Alexander Henderson's indomitable perseverance, Samuel Rutherford's logic and love, Robert Leighton's faculty in Scripture and teaching, Thomas Chalmers' grand conception of the nation's needs and the Church's mission, Henry Drummond's genius for simplicity in communicating the apparent inarticulate.

We are on very common ground with that singular ambition of Thomas Erskine: *"I desire to know more and more the importance of learning Christ, rather than Christianity: the living, loving, almighty Lord of our spirits, rather than the logic about Him."*

The prayer arises that this Diary will have value of eternal consequence to the reader and that it may be an instrument of God's answering to the soul's need for cleansing and the mind's hunger for truth.

John Birkbeck

ACKNOWLEDGMENTS

Scotland has been wonderfully sustained in the publication of devotional material by presses which thought more of the common good than the profit motive in financial records. To them the world owes a debt beyond compute. Many will surely protest their gratitude to God for those who published not reckoning the cost.

Permission to quote extracts for inclusion in this diary has been received from such to whom so much is owed by the searching mind and hungry heart of men and women.

Care has been taken to ascertain that no royalty infringement has taken place. If such has occurred then pardon is sought and the transgression rectified in any subsequent edition.

Acknowledgment is made to the following for permission to reprint copyrighted material:

James Clarke & Co. Ltd.: *Visions of the End*, by Adam C. Welch.
Hodder & Stoughton Limited: *The Quenching Question*, by Hubert L. Simpson; *Heralds of God*, by James S. Stewart; *Isaiah*, by George A. Smith; *Our Perennial Theme*, by G. J. Jeffrey; *The Bread of Life* and *In the Secret of His Presence*, by George H. Knight; *Christ or Chaos*, by E. P. Dickie; *The Significance of Doubt*, by William Dickie; *The Key to the Kingdom*, by James Reid; *The Attainment of Immortality*, by J.Y. Simpson; *Edinburgh Sermons*, by Hugh Black; *Repentence Unto Life*, by William M. Macgregor; *The Christian Faith*, by David H.C. Read.
George Allen & Unwin Ltd.: *Personal Problems of Conduct and Religion*, by J. G. McKenzie.
The British Broadcasting Company: Series on "Why I Believe."
Charles S. Duthie: *God in His World*.
John A. Mackay: *The Divine Drama*.
Marshall, Morgan & Scott Publications Ltd.: *Faith's Title Deeds*, by David M. McIntyre.
Oxford University Press, Inc.: *The Ministry of Worship*, by Oswald B. Milligan; *Asking Them Questions*, by William Manson; *Invitation to Pilgrimage*, by John Baillie; *What Is Salvation?*, by David S. Cairns.
St. Andrew Press: *Why Did Jesus Die?*, by Donald M. Baillie.
The Salvation Army, International Headquarters, London: *The Call to Holiness*, by Frederick Coutts.
SCM Press Ltd.: *The Sayings of Jesus* and *The Mission and Message of Jesus*, by Thomas W. Manson; *Preaching in a Scientific Age*, by A. C. Craig.
James S. Stewart for U.S.A. rights to *Heralds of God*.

CONTENTS

WITH NONE BUT THEE

Alone with none but Thee, my God;
    I journey on my way;
What need I fear, when Thou art near,
    O King of night and day?
More safe am I within Thy hand
    Than if a host did round me stand.

My life I yield to Thy decree,
    And bow to Thy control
In peaceful calm, for from Thine arm
    No power can wrest my soul,
Could earthly omens e'er appal
    A man that heeds the heavenly call!

—Attributed to St. Columba
(521-597)

Translation anonymous

THE PRESENT ONLY IS YOUR OWN

Measuring yourselves by this time last year, are you living nearer to God than you did then, or are your lives laxer, your hearts colder, your prayers fewer and more languid, your attachment to creatures closer? In whatever state you are, recollect that the time is short. God in His mercy has spared you hitherto, to bring forth the fruits of repentance, to live the life of faith, and to keep His holy commandments...the present only is your own.

—Alexander Penrose Forbes
(1817-1875)
Sermon: *The Necessity of Conversion*

Bishop of Brechin

INTO THY PROTECTING HANDS

Into Thy *protecting* hands I commit my spirit, for the *keeping* of it. Life is full of temptations, the world full of snares. Into Thy *tender* hands I commit my spirit for the *comforting* of it. The sorrows of my life may be many, the waters deep, the furnace hot; I may have thick darkness over me soon in which I will lose all my joy. Into Thy *correcting* hands I commit my spirit for the *sanctifying* of it. I am willing to be chastened if only the chastening makes me purer than before. Into Thy *moulding* hands I commit my spirit for the *consecrating* of it. Use me for Thy glory. Into Thy *redeeming* hands I commit my spirit for the *glorifying* of it. So I trust myself entirely and for ever to Thee.

—George H. Knight
(D. 1937)
The Bread of Life

Minister, Garelochhead

I REMIND MY SOUL

Setting forward on my pilgrim march through the year, I remind my soul.... Without holiness no man shall see the Lord.... They who stay with God, either here or hereafter, must sympathise with His aims, must share His likeness, and must be set on fire with His passion for truth and hatred of sin. Else, what community of interest can there be between Him and them? what fellowship of a friendly sort? So let me be certain that my sanctification deepens and increases with every day of the year. It will be a gradual process, a slow and patient ascent. But there will be no doubt of its ending, if I keep steadfast company with Christ. I have only to live habitually in His light, and the light will shine more and more. And one happy morning, in the nearer or farther future, I shall find myself—myself who am so unworthy and so unclean—perfect even as my Father in heaven is perfect.

—Alexander Smellie
(1857-1923)
In the Secret Place

Minister, Original Secession, Carluke

20

MY GIFT FOR THE NEW YEAR

Lord, my body, soul, and spirit, I have long since dedicated to Thee; therefore as the fruits of Thine own grace, receive this as my gift for the new year! As Thou art pleased to increase Thy benefits, so I will my thankfulness, and will continually offer Thee a sacrifice of praise. I cannot give Thee a lamb without blemish, holiness and perfect obedience, but I will give faith, repentance, and love; and yet these must come from Thee. I have nothing of mine own but sin; O that I could part with all the interest I have in that, and then Thou wouldst give me wholly Thyself: to whom I will ascribe all glory evermore. Amen.

> —Lady Anne Murray
> (1622-1670)
> *Prayer: January 1, 1652*

Meditation of Psalm 25

THE REALITY OF THE THING

Some travel on in a covert, cloudy day, and get home by it, having so much light as to know their way, and yet do not at all clearly see the bright and full sunshine of assurance; others have it treading forth at times, and anon under a cloud; and some have it more constantly. But as all meet in the end, so all agree in this in the beginning, that is, in the reality of the thing.

> —Robert Leighton
> (1611-1684)
> *Letters*

Archbishop of Glasgow; Professor; Minister at Dunblane

ABOVE, AROUND, WITHIN

It is the property of the morning star to be the day's harbinger.
Other stars rise and shine and set, and leave the darkness still
behind them. But the morning star is not a child of night but of
the day. With Christ the morning star the victory is decided
from the first, and night can never resume her ancient empire.
The dawn may be overcast, but the day still proceeds.
Gathering clouds may spread and deepen, but the fount of life is
still somewhere in the sky and speaks His presence. In the
blackest, wintriest, stormiest hour of the Christian's pilgrimage, his steps can never be in such darkness as before "the day
dawned and the day star arose in his heart"; for Christ is still
above him, around him, and within him, the hope of glory; and
even when the light of hope seems to fail, there is the light of
memory; and that is daylight compared with the dense
midnight gloom in which he once wandered.

> —John Cairns
> (1818-1892)
> *The Morning Star*

Preacher, Professor, Principal

YOU DID RUN WELL

When the apostle says to them "Ye did run well," he gives them
a great commendation, for in running well there are these things
required—(1)...we must not set our hearts on the world, nor
must we let the dust of it dim our sights, that we see not what is
before us... (2) The way in which we should run is plainly set
down in the Word of God.... There is a way which leads to the
Kingdom of God; Christ is that way. (3) It is a rough,
troublesome, longsome, wearisome way; wherefore we must be
provided for it before we enter the way...to have our feet shod
with the preparation of the gospel of peace. (4) We must lay
aside every weight that presses down; every profit and pleasure
that may hinder us from running fast. (5) We must not go back,
nor may we remember what is behind, nor what we have done,
but always remember what is before us, and so what we have to
do; have our eye aye towards the mark. And if we run so we
shall not be disappointed.

> —Alexander Henderson
> (1583-1646)
> Sermon: *Ye Did Run Well*

Statesman; Preacher, Edinburgh

FALSE, FUTILE, FATAL

A false idea or a diverging step at the outset may lead to a false religion throughout life, to an imperfect and superficial goodness, as one incorrect figure or sign in an equation falsifies both process and result. If the dislocated joint is not properly set, it will never work comfortably; and if the wound is merely skinned over, the disease may be taking its own way underneath, all the more fatally because it is supposed to be removed.

> —Horatius Bonar
> (1808-1889)
> *God's Way of Holiness*

Preacher and Hymnist

WHEN THE ANCHOR IS UP

When the anchor is up and our ship of life has left the land-locked harbour for the open sea, we long, not for calm weather in which to drift at the mercy of every current, but rather to feel the wind in our face; for though it rise to a gale, threatening to drive us far out of our course, we shall bend it to our purpose and beat up the very teeth of it, till we drop anchor in the haven of our desire. Once that haven has our heart, our life must reach it, too. And it is such desire, strengthened by the presence aboard of the Pilot, Who has never lost on the high seas a single ship which was wholly committed to His charge; that will bring us safely through the heaviest weather.

> —John Harry Miller
> (1869-1940)
> *The Safeguard of a Great Desire*

Principal, St. Mary's, St. Andrews

YOU ARE IN SAFE COMPANY

Choose Him, then, my brothers. Choose Him as the Captain of your salvation. Let Him enter your hearts by faith, and let Him dwell continually there. Cultivate a daily intercourse and a growing acquaintance with Him. O, you are in safe company, indeed, when your fellowship is with Him.

> —Thomas Chalmers
> (1780-1847)
> (Last words in last sermon, Kilmany)

Mathematician, Preacher, Leader

MARCH ON, MY SOUL, WITH STRENGTH

March on, my soul, with strength,
    With strength, but not thine own;
The conquest thou shalt gain,
    Through Christ thy Lord alone;
His grace shall nerve thy feeble arm,
His love preserve thee safe from harm.

March on, my soul, with strength,
    In ease thou dar'st not dwell;
High duty calls thee forth;
    Then up, and quit thee well!
Take up thy cross, take up thy sword,
And fight the battles of thy Lord.

> —William Wright
> (1859-1924)
> *Hymn:* "March On, My Soul"

Chemist and Christian Administrator

THE DARKNESS THAT LIGHTS

My soul, why art thou perplexed about the future? Seest thou clouds in tomorrow's sky which thy present strength is inadequate to meet? God has not given thee thy present strength to meet the future, but to meet the present. When thy morrow shall become thy day thou shalt learn thy power over it. Why art thou distressed about the unborn sorrow? Thou thyself art born anew for each new day. Thine armour is freshly burnished to fight each rising sun. In the hour of battle thou wilt laugh at the memory of thy fears.

> —George Matheson
> (1842-1906)

Preacher and Poet

EARNEST SEEKER NEVER DISAPPOINTED

He who, in the faith of a Divine enlightenment, of a spiritual guidance, earnestly seeks to know all that God would teach him, is never disappointed. The light of the inward witness does not fail. The promise of what the "Spirit of truth" will do holds good. Not more sure is the promise that in the outer world, day and night, seed-time and harvest, summer and winter, shall not cease, than that in the world within, the patient, humble, earnest spirit, shall find an ever clearer light encircling it, an ever higher knowledge filling it with strength and peace.

—Robert Hubert Story
(1835-1907)
Sermon: *Christ's Authority*
Minister, Rosneath; Principal, Glasgow University

AWAKENING PROVIDENCES

Words of God come to us with startling power, shedding a sudden light on the unsatisfactory state of things within us; awakening providences break into our lives; bereavements make us lonely, losses make us thoughtful, slow and lingering cares that we cannot shake off force us to cast about for truer comfort and support. Even temptations and falls startle us into fresh thoughts of where we stand and whither we are going. Such things God works oftentimes with men.

—Robert Rainy
(1826-1906)
Sermon: *The Elder Son*
Principal, New College, Edinburgh

SOLEMN TRUTH AND SOLEMN WARNING

"For judgment," said our Lord Himself,—and His words embody a solemn truth, and convey a solemn warning,—"For judgment I am come into this world, that they who see not might see, and that they who see might be made blind." While they who think they see, and imagine that they stand in no need of Divine illumination, are left to wander in darkness, they who are sensible of their blindness, and who desire, however feebly, yet honestly, the teaching of the Spirit of God, will be led and guided into all truth. Taking the Word of God as a lamp unto their feet, and a light unto their path, and looking up to Him who inspired it, they shall be enabled to behold wondrous things out of His law, and shall know of the doctrine of Christ, that it is indeed of God, and fitted to make men wise unto salvation.

—Robert Williamson
(1819-1902)
Sermon: *The Heart and the Understanding*

Minister, Ascog

LIGHT IN WHICH I SEE MEN

The light of truth in which I see God as my Father is the light in which I see men as my brethren.... In the light of love which we have in Christ not only will God have His proper preciousness to us, but men will also have theirs. Love will go out to me as to God.... If we refuse to be in Christ the brothers of men we cannot in Christ be the sons of God.

—John McLeod Campbell
(1800-1872)

Minister, Rhu

ONLY KEEP ON...

God will not withhold from you His faithful help if He finds you constant and patient in trying to do His will in spite of many discouragements. Only keep on praying, keep on watching, keep on working; and He will watch with you, and work in you and enable you to do what looked once quite impossible to you. Be not content with a life of commonplace morality, but seek also the life of spiritual power and holiness; and doubt not that He will back you up, for this is the very purpose of His grace, that you should adorn the doctrine of God your Saviour in all things. Be not discouraged, then, either because it is so high a calling or because you have failed, but trust in Him and be of good heart, for His grace will be sufficient for you.

—Walter Chalmers Smith
(1824-1908)
Sermon: *Glorifying God*
Minister, Free High, Edinburgh

I MET A MAN!

It came to me as it does to most—in a flash and as a result of long and serious thought. I got moral certainty in place of a defective logical proof. *I met a Man.* ECCE HOMO! He did not speak to me in abstract syllogisms. He revealed the grace and truth of God in a human life...Without Him I would still be groping. At that stage of my life I gave up the study of law for the Gospel and entered the Church. In this change I was guided, compelled by that revelation of the Christ when He said: "You have not chosen me—but I have chosen you!" Life would be a tragedy—and mockery of all that God has done for us in Christ—if life was bounded by this time and space world. I must believe that a new order of life will be mine. Eternal Life, which is something more than endless existence, is one of the consistent promises of the New Testament. It means a full life, spiritual felicity and an unwearied service.

—John White
(1867-1951)
Why I Believe
Minister, Moderator, Statesman

27

CHRIST—THE MAN

If He were not a man, but only the apparition of a man, a superior being who for a certain end and purpose had clothed Himself with human form; if He had not a reasonable soul, the consequences cannot be denied. His human feelings and affections were but an assumed fiction to carry the end which His mission had in view; and His sufferings and His death were a phantasmagoria played off before the eyes of men, but by no means entering into the vitals of human sympathy, nor proceeding from the communion and love of human kind, nor answering any end of comforting human suffering, and interceding for human weakness.

—Edward Irving
(1792-1834)
Doctrine of the Incarnation Opened
Minister, Regent Square, London

OUR INVINCIBLE EVASIVENESS

When shall we be free from duplicity in dealing with the things of the spirit? When shall our worship be in spirit and in truth? When shall our praise rise from the heart and our prayer be never a mere uttering of unreal words? When shall we have learned to believe God's promises, to put the aid He offers us to full proof, and in a word, to take Him and His will and mercy seriously? Our invincible evasiveness here is our worst misery, as it is also the source of the pithlessness and ineffectiveness of our lives. We believe, but we disbelieve also; we accept some portion of His goodness but much we leave alone; we do His will in part, and even more we live at ease. When shall our heart be right with God, and our life, lived under one dominant motive be free from distraction and fretting? When shall our eye be single and the whole body full of light?

—Alexander Martin
(1857-1946)
Sermon: *The Armour of Light*
Preacher; Principal, New College, Edinburgh

THE SECRET OF SECRETS

Man's face is a strange mixture of the flush of pride and the blush of shame....Sometimes we are deceived by our own hearts, perhaps just where we are surest of ourselves, or we may be taken unawares, or there may be some vanity or paltry shame not eradicated. Life is too complex, too difficult for us. But the secret of secrets is the Master's promise to be with us to the end of the world, a pillar of fire in the night of our adversity and a pillar of cloud in the day of our prosperity. We need to know nothing so much as our own weakness and the Lord's strength.

—John Wood Oman
(1860-1939)
Sermon: *Christian Contentment*
Professor of Systematic Theology, Principal,
Presbyterian College of England

FIND A GREATER WONDER

Seek where ye will and say whether ye can find a greater wonder in all the world than Christ.

If there be but one of you, He will be the second. If there be but two of you, He will be the third. Ye shall never lack for company.

Without Him the most of mosts is nothing. With Him the least of leasts is All.

—Covenanting Preachers
Selected extracts

WALK IN A CIRCLE OF LIGHT

Mine, like other men, be days of battle, but every morning I open the window for my King's Grace, and every evening I sleep upon the pillow of His love and care.

If a man does his own will he walks with a shadow on the heart, but if with Christ's power in thee, thou doest God's will, thou shalt walk in a circle of light. (9th century)

The world cannot satisfy the soul because the soul is bigger than the world.

—Unknown Celtic Saints
Selected Extracts

DURING WORKING HOURS

I must fear to teach what I am not seen to be.... I have known very many men in the religious life who devoted themselves wholeheartedly to inward meditation while they were engaged in physical labour, and the food of the life-giving scriptures, which they received from reading during the cloister time, they redigested during working hours, and thus fixed it more firmly in their memory.

—Adam of Dryburgh
(*c.* 1140-*c.* 1212)
De Ord

GIVE ME THAT BREAD!

Lord Jesus, thou art the bread of life: give me that bread which shall feed me to life everlasting; and grant, that as I cannot live without a dependence upon thee, so may I never desire to live without it, but that the eyes of my soul may be always looking towards thee, and receive with thankfulness my temporal and spiritual food from thy hands. O that I could give my heart entirely to thee! Lord, I am a poor defiled wretch; but it is by thy blood I must be cleansed, whose I am, and to whom I do resign myself, soul and body, and all that is mine. This is what gratitude obliges me to, since he gave himself for sinners, of whom I am the chief.

—Anne, Countess of Seafield
(1672-1707)
Meditation on the Lord's Prayer

TRUTH AND LOVE

I can live without health. I can live without creeds and churches, without all that distinguishes a gentleman from a man; but two things I cannot live without—Truth and Love. The want of truth blinds me, and the want of love freezes me and I die.

—John Stuart Blackie
(1809-1895)
Lecture to Students
Professor, Edinburgh University

STAR OF MY MORNING

Lord Christ, you are the only person in my universe of knowledge who can help me. You are the only being who can take my past and with the veil of your forgiving love hide it forever from my eyes. You are the only force who can quicken my paralyzed and irresolute will. You are the star of my morning and the light of my world.

—Alistair Maclean
(1885-1936)
Radiant Certainty
Minister at Daviot, Invernesshire

TURN THE DISCOVERY OVER

In order to meditate, we must call to remembrance the things we have learned, and we must seek to store our minds with new and fresh truths, but neither of these is meditation itself. To remember a fact is not to ponder it.... A passage remembered is so much food laid up in a storehouse; a passage meditated is so much food eaten, and digested, and incorporated with ourselves. The mere student has found his end when he has apprehended a conception, laid hold on an idea, demonstrated a fact, established a law; the meditative man finds his end only when he was turned the discovery over and over in his mind, and viewed it in all its bearings and relations, has questioned it as to its uses and worth, has inwrought it with his own being, and made it part of his own mind—the fruitful parent of new thoughts and new affections.

—William Lindsay Alexander
(1808-1884)
Religious Meditation
Minister, Edinburgh

LET ME...

Let me read by the light of the Spirit Prayerfully, Thoughtfully, with increasing interest.... Let me meditate in the Strength of Thy Spirit and with close thought, revolving much Thy Holiness and Love.... Let me pray in the Spirit.... perseveringly; fervently, trustfully, joyfully, humbly, abounding with love, large-mindedly, and do Thou suggest the subjects of my prayers. Let my heart rise continuously and readily to thankfulness, and let the stain of ingratitude which marks my fallen nature, be felt more abhorrently, and by Thy grace effaced. Let praise come to be the spontaneous language of my heart, and no longer a feeble and intermittent effort.

—Lady Blanche Balfour
(1825-1872)
Prayers

HOPE IN CHRIST

I desire this day to humble myself before God, and to bless Him as my creator, who called me into being at first; who has been my preserver in the midst of many dangers; and who hath ever since my birth, loaded me with tender mercies and favours. But above all, I would bless His holy name, that He hath not left me in the state of alienation from Him in which I was by nature, but that He hath of His own free grace and mercy, brought me out of darkness and shown me the glorious light of His gospel, and caused me to hope for salvation through Jesus Christ.

—Williamina Maxwell, Lady
Glenorchy
(1741-1786)
Diary—September 2, 1765

FAITH AND INCREDULITY

Faith is the root of all good; incredulity is the root of all evil. Faith maketh God and man good friends; incredulity maketh them foes. Faith bringeth God and man together; incredulity sundereth them. All that faith doth pleaseth God. Faith only maketh a man good and righteous; incredulity only maketh him unjust and evil. Faith maketh a man a member of Christ; incredulity maketh him a member of the devil.

—Patrick Hamilton
(1500-1528)

Scholar and Martyr

NONE IS BORN A CHRISTIAN

The awful and the amazing thing about the Bible is that it asks us to stand upon our feet, responsible beings with whom God is going to converse, people to whom He is going to commit His counsels. "Son of man, stand upon thy feet, and I will speak to thee." What other book speaks with accents like these?

None of us is born a Christian. We are born with certain Christian advantages, and certain Christian associations, but every generation has got to be born anew. How will it take place? We become Christian when we hear and accept that Word which at the same time is so simple and winsome and kind, and so awful and imperious and challenging—The Word of God. And when we hear and answer that infallible Word of God, which never led men astray, then we are born again.

—George Sinclair Gunn
(1900-1961)
Sermon: *God's Word*

Minister, Broughton Place, Edinburgh

AS FAITH INCREASES

As faith increases, all the graces of the Christian life increase; piety becomes deeper, hope brighter, and love more pure; joy in the heart is augmented, heavenly desires are quickened, holiness becomes more predominant, the mind becomes more penetrated and imbued with the heavenly Spirit; and thus assurance of our own personal salvation is increasingly, and that on solid and Scriptural grounds, conveyed to us; until at length, the victory of faith being complete, we shall "receive the end of our faith, even the salvation of our souls."

> —William Lindsay Alexander
> (1808-1884)
> Sermon: *Assurance of Faith
> and Assurance of Salvation*

Minister, Edinburgh

A HEAVY PRICE TO PAY

But there is a price we have to pay for this faith. That is what we sometimes forget. It is not a faith we can have on easy terms. It is a delicate, fragile, sensitive thing, and you can easily lose it. The price you have to pay is to practise the presence of God in your life as Jesus did. When you get out of practice, the faith goes. It is a heavy price to pay. It means discipline and submission and surrender. You need to be very quiet to hear the footfall of God's presence in your life, and often we live such noisy lives that we fail to hear it.

> —Robert Guy Ramsay
> (1895-   )
> Sermon: *Does God Care?*

Minister, Hillhead Baptist Church, Glasgow

HIS VISION IS OUR FAITH

There is nothing arbitrary in this sublime faith, nothing that does not rise out of the human order, nothing that is mere import from the world of fancy or wild belief. The faith is the translation of fact into thought and speech. The eyes of Christ pass over and through the order of the universe, and His vision is our faith. Man is the interpreter of nature; religion is the interpreter of man; Christianity is the interpreter of religion; and God the Father is the interpreter of Christianity.

—George Angier Gordon
(1853-1929)
Sermon: *Man in the Image of God*
Pastor, Old South Church, Boston, Mass.

THROUGH FAITH, HOPE, LOVE

Jesus will never forsake them that truly love him. Though their love be but a feeble spark, he will not suffer it to be quenched amid the trials and troubles of this life, but will watch over it and yet fan it into a flame. Though their faith be weak, he will give growing distinctness to its views and confidence in the promises it embraces, and make them strong in its exercise, giving glory to God. Though hope may now struggle feebly with doubt and fear, it shall yet fix its anchor firmly within the veil, and comfort the soul that is tossed with tempest, with the sure prospect of an entrance into the desired haven.

—James Henderson
(1787-1858)
Sermon: *Evidences of Love to Jesus*
Minister at Galashiels

HE ONLY SAYS "LOOK!"

Act faith if you do not feel it....Throw yourself in His direction, even though you cannot reach Him....He does not say "See": He only says "Look"...that is all you have to do with, He will take care of the rest....It is very simple—keep *looking;* He will take care of the *seeing.*

—Alexander Whyte
(1837-1921)
Minister, St. George's, Edinburgh

February 8

REASON GROWN COURAGEOUS

Faith is not concerned with believing historical or other propositions on inadequate evidence. *It is reason grown courageous*, the spirit which inspires martyrs, the confidence that right must inevitably triumph, that all things work together for good to those who love God.

> —John Wood Oman
> (1860-1939)
> Letter: *The Times—February 8, 1934*

Professor of Systematic Theology,
Principal, Presbyterian College of England

February 9

ESSENTIAL TO PERFECTION

The more man advances in culture the more true will it be that faith is essential to his perfection and his success. Faith widens and quickens and regulates man's intellectual activity. Faith, as an intellectual conviction assents to the truth. Faith, therefore, cannot exist without some activity of the intellect. Faith is necessary to man's happiness, and I have always observed, that there is no lasting happiness without faith.

> —Alexander Balmain Bruce
> (1831-1889)
> *St. Paul's Conception of Christianity*

Preacher and Professor

February 10

CHRISTIAN WAY TO GOD

The way to God is not primarily a psychological process. It is not a geographical route; nor a religious hierarchy; nor a holy shrine; nor esoteric knowledge. The Christian way to God is a person who becomes the object of that belief and commitment which is called faith. In Jesus Christ God and man meet. On the one hand, Christ is the embodiment of all that the Bible means by the word "grace," that is, the approach of God to man for his redemption, in which all the resources of deity are made available for man. On the other hand, He is the object of commitment in thought and in life which we call faith.

> —John Alexander Mackay
> (1889-   )
> *A Preface to Christian Theology*

Missionary; former President, Princeton Theological Seminary

BECOME RECEPTIVE

The more I think of the teachings of our Lord concerning faith, the more I have the sense that around us there is a world of power, and love, and strength, and life, and that the thing we need to learn above all else is to become receptive to it. Let us realise that it may be that we are also face to face with the greatest potentiality of getting to know God that we have ever had in our lives, and our victory depends upon our opening our minds to Him in order that He may come in to flood them with His strength, and life.

> —David Smith Cairns
> (1862-1946)
> *Friends and the War*

Principal, Christ's College, Aberdeen

MAKE MUCH OF QUIET THINGS

True religion is a silent energy, and if a soul is full of excitement and tumult, faith and hope cannot find entrance. Let us make much of all quiet things if we would have our souls keep their sanity and sweetness in this difficult time. Let us make much of the quiet sights of nature, quiet books, quiet music, quiet friendship, quiet home life, quiet meditation, quiet worship, the companionship of the quiet Christ and communion with the quiet Spirit. Let the Good Shepherd of our pilgrimage lead us again and again to green pastures and still waters.

> —John Hunter
> (1849-1917)
> Sermon: *Faith in Stormy Days*

Congregationalist Minister and Devotionalist, Trinity, Glasgow

FAITH IS DEEPER THAN DESPAIR

No man will have faith who does not acknowledge his need of faith. Faith is light from heaven falling upon a bankrupt spirit: the still small voice after the earthquake and the fire and the mighty wind. Faith is something deeper than despair.

> —John Alexander Hutton
> (1868-1947)
> *Warrack Lectures 1921*

Preacher; Editor, *British Weekly*

FAITH IS GOD'S HIGHWAY

Your faith in God is God's opportunity. Your faith is God's highway and along this highway God is forever marching, bringing you those powers which you need if you really are wishful to make living a tremendously glad and successful experience. Your faith is a key in God's fingers. With it He opens the iron doors of doubt and ignorance and in a moment His light comes triumphing and streaming in. You believe, and instantly receive, the loveliest gifts: the mightiest powers, the most enriching capacities.

> —Alistair Maclean
> (1885-1936)
> Sermon: *The Victory That Is
> Not Enough*

Minister at Daviot, Invernesshire

LOVE LIGHTENS HEAVIEST BURDENS

The Christian lives not under a reign of terror, but of love. He obeys not from fear but from affection. He does not tremble like a slave, but he has the free, happy look of a child. And the duties of Christianity are not extorted from an aroused and alarmed conscience, they are the freewill offerings of a loving heart. We are willing workers for Christ, but labour in His service is felt to be no drudgery, for love lightens the heaviest burdens.

> —John Cunningham
> (1819-1893)
> Sermon: *The Religion of Love*

Minister, Crieff North; Principal of St. Mary's, St. Andrews

AN INFORMED CONSCIENCE

Let then the Conscience be well informed by the Word; let its dictates according thereunto, be tenderly complied with, and none of them counteracted; and let all its checks, challenges, accusations, with its answers, testimonies and excuses, according to their respective grounds and reasons, be carefully listened to and admitted; in a word, let all study once to have a good conscience, and to be always exercised to keep it void of offence against God and toward men: And then great honour and glory would redound to God, the Lord and Sovereign of the Conscience; suitable and due deference would be given to his Word, as that whereby the Conscience is rightly informed; the peace of men's own Consciences would flow as a river; the offending and stumbling of others would be much prevented; the profession of the Doctrine of the Gospel of Christ would be much adorned and beautified.

—James Durham
(1622-1658)
Heaven and Hell, 1685

Minister, Glasgow

APPLY THESE TESTS

The fundamental religious test is: Do we hold fast our faith in God, and believe that, though clouds and thick darkness are round about Him, He has shined upon us in Jesus Christ, and given us to trust His wisdom and His love? The fundamental moral test is whether the centre of gravity has shifted in our lives, and we have learned to ask, not where we can find profit or pleasure, but how we can be of some use. Let us ask our conscience to apply these tests and deliver a verdict. Self-knowledge is difficult, but the conscience has moments of insight in which it wonderfully justifies its title of the Vice-gerent of God.

—William Paterson Paterson
(1860-1939)
Sermon: *In the Day of Ordeal*

Professor of Divinity, Edinburgh

SET YOURSELVES IN HIS SIGHT

Let Him who, for sinners, shed all His most precious blood at Jerusalem, obtain this of you; that you will take one day each of you alone, from morn to evening, forbearing both meat and drink, and go apart rather into some quiet room in a house, or unto some part of the fields, where you may be most quiet, and having beforehand marked in the Bible such places as are fit to be read at such a time, as also, having somewhat searched your way towards God, and His ways toward you, there set yourselves in His sight, spending the time in confession of sins, and prayer for pardon and grace to serve Him, and save your own souls.

—John Livingston
(1603-1672)
Letter—October 1671, to the
People at Ancrum
Minister at Ancrum; Exiled to Rotterdam

THAT IS GOD'S WORD

The world is forever busying itself with what it is pleased to call "burning questions." Some of them do not burn very long. Others turn out to be only finger-burning questions. Some of them throw out crackling sparks; some produce little else than clouds of pungent and obscuring smoke; while most burn while they last with a good deal of heat, but afford wondrous little light.... We are ready with many questions, questions with a touch of complaint in them, with a note of self-excuse, with more than a hint of self-satisfaction. God is ready with His answer: "What think ye of Christ?" That is His Word, His last word.

—Hubert Louis Simpson
(1880-1953)
The Quenching Question
Minister, Westbourne, Glasgow

LOOK AT YOUR LIFE

If you have found hollowness and dissatisfaction almost everywhere in life, is this not a reason for you now learning of Him and truly studying and adopting His spirit? Can you look at your life as a whole and be perfectly content with it? Are you prepared to exhibit it in its inward principles and secret motives, in all that has characterised it, and to justify it to yourself and to all? Are you willing that the whole of it should be spent as you have spent a part?

—Marcus Dods
(1834-1909)
Sermon: *The Great Invitation*
Professor of New Testament Exegesis, Edinburgh

SEARCH AND SEE

If any of you are strangers to Christ, it is due in all likelihood to "one thing." Many obstacles may have appeared to hinder you; but the fatal obstruction is at one point, one secret sin, or one proud imagination. Search and see. There may be many cobwebs woven across the closed door of the heart; but draw the bolt, and everything else will give way. Draw the bolt, and the Lord who is knocking at the door will enter. And if He come in, what shall we have? "One thing": but it is everything. It is the good part which shall not be taken away, the enduring treasure which shall never waste away. It is unsearchable riches, unspotted righteousness, unfaltering peace, unspeakable joy.

—Donald Fraser
(1826-1892)
Sermon: *One Thing*
Minister, Montreal, Canada; Marylebone, London

USE THAT SAME ARGUMENT

Those that have not another argument to plead with God but their sinful helpless condition and frailty, despair not; use that same argument and it may prevail. Be not discouraged, it is a forcible argument with God, if we have an interest in the covenant of grace; for we must not look to ourselves what we are, but at the same time we must look to God what He is. Oh that we knew these two things aright!

> —Lord Alexander Brodie
> (1617-1680)
> *Diaries*

Laird of Brodie

IMPROPERLY YOURS

A lady once said to me, "The more I see of myself, I see nothing so properly mine as my sin." I said to her, "Well, you do not see deep enough. There is something far more properly yours than your sin; and your sin is improperly yours. It is a blot in your being, which, if you do not get quit of it, will never cease to be *unnatural* to you. No; the image of God is more properly yours, though you had no share in the production of it."

> —John Duncan
> (1796-1870)
> *Colloquia Peripatetica*

Professor of Hebrew, Edinburgh

ORIGIN OF SELF-RIGHTEOUSNESS

We are never wholly disinterested in our conduct; we have always an eye to some personal advantage, and therefore, we naturally consider it necessary to possess some merit to entitle us to the favor of God. Even when we talk of mercy, it is not perfectly free and gratuitous; but a blessing which we hope God will bestow in consideration of some duty which we have performed, or some evil from which we have abstained—such is the origin of self-righteousness.

—James Alexander Haldane
(1786-1851)
The Pharisee and the Publican
Independent evangelist

AFTER GOD'S OWN HEART

You may sacrifice yourself like St. Simeon on the top of his pillar, to uselessness and vanity. Self-sacrifice for its own sake is not necessarily noble or beautiful: but self-sacrifice for the high end of witnessing for God's spiritual kingdom, for God's moral order, for God's universal goodwill toward men,—self-sacrifice, carried out in personal purity and charity and unselfish endeavour to do good, is after God's own heart. He loves it, because He sees in it the repetition in other lives (though at an interval almost infinite) of the sacrifice of His own Son.

—Robert Hubert Story
(1835-1907)
Religion and Revelation
Minister, Rosneath; Principal, Glasgow University

LOSS OF ALL FINER SENSIBILITIES

For it is vain to think that you can do evil, and reap no consequences from it; that you may commit sin, and have done with it. The hand of the dyer is not more certainly imbued with the colours with which he works, than the soul takes on the complexion of the thoughts with which it indulges. Sin finds a man out by an accumulation of sinfulness, through the hardening of his heart and conscience, through the enfeebling of the will, through the loss of all the finer sensibilities of the mind, and the general lowering of the whole tone of character.

—Andrew Bruce Davidson
(1831-1902)
Jacob at Peniel

Professor of Theology, Glasgow

LET NOT THE WISEST...IMAGINE

Let not the wisest, the best, and the most confirmed Christians imagine that they do not stand in need of watching and praying that they enter not into temptation. Even in you the flesh is weak. Sin hath not dominion over you; but the remains of sin are still within you. Your sanctification is begun at your conversion; but it will not be finished until you finish your course in this world. You are babes or young men in Christ; but you are not yet arrived at the full stature of perfect men in Christ. You have received grace; but you have not yet received glory from God.

—Bryce Johnston
(1747-1805)
On the Nature of Temptation

Minister of Holywood

THINK OF THE...

And when inward corruption, or an ensnaring world, or spiritual enemies, interfere to weaken your faith and seduce you into sin, think of your obligations—think of the grace by which alone you can be saved—think of the wounds by which Jesus takes away your transgressions—think of the love of that Holy Spirit whom your backsliding will grieve—think of the sorrows of those who, desiring you to be their crown and joy and rejoicing, must mourn and weep when they see your falling away—think of the endless ages that lie before you; and let all these considerations put their interdict upon every unbelieving thought—upon every unholy desire—upon every forboding gratification.

—Andrew Thomson
(1779-1831)
Sermon: *Salvation by Grace*
Minister, St. George's, Edinburgh

NO OTHER WORTHINESS

Our Lord requireth no other worthiness on our part but that we unfeignedly acknowledge our naughtiness and our imperfections....It enables the enfeebled soul to look steadily at the divine light, to breathe deeply of the familiar air, till God calls us, too, to Himself, and makes us glad with the beauty of His unveiled presence.

—John Knox
(1505-1572)
On Holy Communion
Reformer; Minister at St. Giles, Edinburgh

VILEST SINNER AND RIPEST SAINT

I say then to all, confess your sins to God through Jesus Christ who, by His death, has become the Propitiation for the sins of the whole world. To the vilest sinner I say it, and also to the ripest saint. Would you *enter into* fellowship with God? Confess your sins. Would you *maintain* your fellowship with God? Confess your sins. Let *all* confess, with the most perfect assurance that God will forgive them their sins, and will cleanse them from all unrighteousness. And sooner would the throne of righteousness be overturned, and God Himself cease to be, than that He should either cast out of His fellowship, or refuse to admit into His fellowship, one who makes unreserved confession of His sins.

> —James John Glen Kippen
> (1846-1904)
> Sermon: *Confession of Sins*

Minister at Pitcairngreen, Perth

WHEN PENITENCE TAKES OVER

But where the feelings of penitence take possession of the mind, they naturally and unavoidably alter the disposition and have a direct influence in reforming the conduct. The stings of conscience, the meltings of sorrow, the prayers for pardon, the solemn renunciations of sin and the resolutions of amendment, all of which are included in penitence prove so many powerful arguments, to resist the violence of those passions which have produced so much pain. They will probably abate the strength and impetuosity of unlawful desires; they will certainly prove natural curbs and restraints to prevent us from indulging these.

> —John Farquhar
> (1732-1768)
> *Sermon IX (Psalm 51:7) (1772)*

Minister at Nigg, Aberdeen

IT IS A RETURN

Repentance is not striving to bring one's conduct into line with the Law or with the higher righteousness demanded by Jesus. Neither is it a painful scrutiny of one's motives with a view to substituting, let us say, unselfish for selfish motives. It is a return of the whole personality to God, a submission of the will to His will, the acceptance of His authority.... The change itself is made possible by the new experience of God as Jesus reveals Him, that is, as the merciful loving Father who seeks and saves the lost.

—Thomas Walter Manson
(1893-1958)
The Mission and Message of Jesus
Professor of Biblical Criticism and Exegesis, Manchester

THAT IMPRESSION OF SIN

Repentance is an adequate sense not of our folly, nor of our misery, but of our sin: as the New Testament puts it, it is repentance toward God. It is the consciousness of what our sin is to Him: of the wrong it does to His holiness, of the wound which it inflicts on His love.... It is the simple truth that that sorrow of heart, that healing and sanctifying pain in which sin is really put away, is not ours in independence of God; it is a saving grace which is begotten in the soul under that impression of sin which it owes to the revelation of God in Christ.

—James Denney
(1856-1917)
The Atonement and the Modern Mind
Professor of Theology, Glasgow

REUNION OF LIFE ... FORGIVENESS

There is no pause between the penitence and the forgiveness. Into the soul opened by penitence, there comes the waiting Spirit of Christ, and that reunion of life is forgiveness. The words "Thy sins are forgiven thee" carry with them the command "Arise." They are but parts of the one restoration of life.

—Cosmo Gordon Lang
(1864-1945)
Archbishop of Canterbury

THE FIRST STEP—CONTRITION

Remember that you should not address yourself to this Table unless you find your hearts in some way prepared. The first step in preparation is contrition, sorrowing for sin, a feeling of your own sins, in which you have offended so gracious a God....But where there is displeasure for sin, an intention to do better, an earnest sorrow and a yearning to receive the thing which you desire, then in that soul where God has placed this desire for Christ, God's spirit is at work, and Christ will enter in.

—Robert Bruce
(1554-1631)
The Sacraments in General

Minister, St. Giles, Edinburgh

WHAT IS REPENTANCE?

What is repentance? It is a change of mind; it is having new thoughts, another heart about things, but above all about the Author of all, about God. It is the determined resolution, the settled resolve to think His thoughts, and walk in His ways. It is the anguish and effort not even in thought to return to the old places, and repeat the old sins. It is the softening that comes about the heart, the sinking at the knees, the clasping the fair feet of Christ, and covering them with what sweetness a new love can lay open upon the lips, and what bitterness an old life can bring to the eyes.

—Robert William Barbour
(1854-1891)
Thoughts

Minister, Cults, Aberdeenshire

ASHAMED TO APPLY TO CHRIST

Now I will bless the Lord that ever there was such as thing as the free grace of God and a free ransom for sold souls; only, alas, guiltiness makes me ashamed to apply to Christ, and makes me think it pride in me to put out my unclean and withered hand to such a Saviour! But it is neither shame nor pride for a drowning man to swim to a rock, nor for the ship-broken soul to run himself ashore upon Christ.

> —Samuel Rutherford
> (1600-1661)
> *Letters*

Preacher and Devotional Writer, St. Andrews

THE GUILT WHICH WE CONTRACT

We see, then, that the guilt which we contract is not a fate riveted upon the soul, but an incubus, a burden which may be rolled off, though oftentimes with painful effort, from our shoulders. God desireth not the death of the wicked, but rather that they should turn to Him and live; that is, attain to the true and pure and higher life. He will judge the world in righteousness, and render to every man according to his deeds, but He pities and forgives the penitent, and extends to them His hand that they may walk with trembling, faltering steps in the ways of holiness.

> —William Mackintosh
> (1821-1894)
> Sermon: *The Renovating Power of Christianity*

Minister, Buchanan

ONLY BY REPENTANCE AND FAITH

Brother, I have never read in the Scripture of God of such a place as purgatory, nor yet believe I that there is anything that may purge the souls of men but the blood of Christ Jesus, which ransom standeth in no earthly thing, nor in soul-mass, nor dirigie, nor in gold, nor silver, but only by repentance of sins, and faith in the blood of Jesus Christ.

> —Patrick Hamilton
> (1500-1528)
> *At his trial for heresy*

Scholar and Martyr

WE SHALL FIND HIM

Let us follow on to know the Lord, and we *shall find Him as a dawn prepared,* a delightful phrase, which is a little gospel in itself.... Our day is nearly done, men say, and we are now bound to travel on in deepening gloom, to darkness and eclipse and defeat. It is not so, says Hosea; I tell you of One who can give you the dew of the morning again, and an outlook over the radiant possibilities of a whole new day.... His prevailing mercy admits of no delay, and is not checked even by the gathered power of years of evil living.

—William Malcolm Macgregor
(1861-1944)
Repentance Unto Life
Professor, New Testament, Glasgow

THE CUP OF FORGIVENESS

Nothing is more oppressive than unforgiven sin. Ever and anon our conscience rattles the chain to let us hear that we are in bondage to some unlovely thing that we try to hide even from ourselves. It is a sickening enslavement. But, don't you see, the taunting force has passed over, and we can go free from its intimidating recollection, because the Divine Host welcomes us as His guests and holds out the cup of forgiveness.

—Arthur A. Cowan
(1883-1959)
Sermon: *The Banquet of Liberty*
Minister, Innerleithen

NOTHING BUT THINE
EVERLASTING MERCY

O Righteous Father, we have nothing to set betwixt us and our sins but Thine everlasting mercy, freely offered in Thy Son Jesus Christ. For His sake, therefore, grant us forgiveness: take from us our stony hearts, and give us hearts of flesh, quick to reverence and observe Thy Word; through the same Jesus Christ our Lord.

—John Knox
(1505-1572)
Prayer
Reformer; Minister at St. Giles, Edinburgh

GOODNESS DELIGHTETH TO FORGIVE

If I have wandered in those paths
    Of life I ought to shun—
As something, loudly, in my breast,
    Remonstrates I have done—

Thou know'st that Thou hast formed me
    With passions wild and strong;
And list'ning to their witching voice
    Has often led me wrong.

Where with intention I have err'd,
    No other plea I have,
But, Thou art good; and Goodness still
    Delighteth to forgive.

         —Robert Burns
         (1759-1796)
         A Prayer in the Prospect of Death

Ploughman Poet

JESUS NEVER PROMISED

Jesus Christ never promised to keep any man that his sins should be forgiven, while his heart remained in a state of alienation from God. Those who have their sins forgiven through His name, are those who are united unto Him as their Head, the members of His spiritual kingdom.... Our blessed Saviour does not say to us, Come unto me, and I will obtain for you the forgiveness of your sins, whatever your conduct may be, if you will but trust in Me as your Redeemer from condemnation; but He says, Come unto Me, and I will give you the power to become the sons of God, not only the objects of His fatherly love, but also a willing people unto Him.

         —William Ramsay
         (1822-1850)
         Sermon: *The Offence of the Cross*

Minister, Guthrie

SAY UNTO US

Have mercy upon us, Father in Heaven; for within us is a remembrance no tears can wash away. Upon us lies a load heavy and grievous: the load of duties unfulfilled, of words unspoken, or spoken untruthfully, idly, unlovingly; of evil thoughts re-appearing again and again, even as they were first admitted into the heart; of talents hidden; of days wasted for ever. O cleanse us from all our sins; from those we have not observed, and those we have forgotten. Say unto us: Be of good cheer, thy sins are forgiven thee. Say unto us: My grace is sufficient for thee. And bring us from beneath the shadow of our guilt unto our Father's House in peace; through Jesus Christ our Lord.

—James Rankine
(1831-1902)
Minister, Muthil, Perthshire

HARDEST KIND OF FORGIVENESS

I am inclined to think that to forgive one's self is sometimes the hardest kind of forgiveness. Self is the inmost entrenchment at which the unforgiving spirit makes its last stand....To the stern, self-disciplined man, to a woman who has deep and conscientious feelings, it is no easy matter to forgive ourselves....Many a wrecked life is due to this unforgiveness of self. The prodigal would never have come home had he been unable to forgive himself....And this unwillingness to forgive one's self is the last refuge of the selfish spirit.

—Thomas Martin Lindsay
(1843-1914)
Sermon: *Forgiving One Another*
Principal, Theological College, Glasgow

LAY DOWN ... TAKE UP

Behold the Cross, the symbol of peace, the meetingplace of souls for pardon, the starting point of communion with God. Come, be ye reconciled. Lay down your enmity, and take up divine friendship. Lay down your guilt, and take up a free pardon. Lay down the flesh, and take up the Spirit. Lay down sight, and take up faith. Lay down the world, and take up Heaven. Lay down your self-righteous works, and take up grace. Lay down sin, and take up salvation. Lay down sorrow and despair, and take up joy and hope. Lay down time, and take up eternity. All, all this is free to you at the Cross of Christ.

—John H. Fraser
(1823-1884)
Sermon before the
General Assembly, 1870

Minister, Rosskeen Free Church

THE OUTSTRETCHED HANDS

In the presence of that Cross and Passion we are all sinners. There are no righteous people. And now, on this Passion Sunday, from that Cross of Christ, God Himself is stretching out His hands to us, appealing to us to repent and return to Him and be forgiven and make a new beginning. St. Paul expressed that appeal when he said, in the words of our text: "God commends His own love toward us in that, while we were yet sinners, Christ died for us." And three centuries later another great saint expressed it in words of magnificent symbolism, when he said; "It is only on a cross that a man dies with outstretched hands."

—Donald Macpherson Baillie
(1887-1954)
Why Did Jesus Die?

Professor of Theology, St. Andrews

SEEK TO REMEMBER CHRIST

When all else fails to impress us, when life ceases either to inspire us with hope or fear, when our heart is shut to warning, to hope, to remonstrance, to reasoning, to remembrance of Christ bleeding, suffering, agonising, dying for us finds the heart and makes us human again. If you have strength for nothing else, you can fall at the foot of the cross; if your faith is limited and feeble, you can yet believe in the death of Christ, in the love that prompted it, in the redemption it aimed at.... Do not seek in the first place to pray for pardon, or to secure peace with God, or to be delivered from sorrow, or to seek great things for yourself; but seek to remember Christ, to let your mind settle upon His pure compassion, His untold anguish, and in your heart to say, "He loved me, and gave Himself for me."

—Marcus Dods
(1834-1909)
Sermon: *In Remembrance of Me*
Professor of New Testament Exegesis, Edinburgh

EVERLASTING NAY—YEA

In the Cross of Jesus Christ the inmost nature of evil and the inmost nature of divine redemptive love were both revealed. It is there that the supreme crisis in both the life of God and man took place. Evil in all its concreteness and personal reality challenged Christ and what He stood for, consummating the historic tragedy of the Cross. This challenge was of the nature of an "Everlasting Nay" hurled at God Himself. To this challenge God in Christ responded with an "Everlasting Yea," enduring the onslaught of evil, suffering the consequences of outraged righteousness, making an end of sin and its power over man, and, in the resurrection, triumphing over all that stood between man and his true destiny.

—John Alexander Mackay
(1889-   )
The Divine Drama
Missionary; former President, Princeton Theological Seminary

RETURN TO THE SHEPHERD

Are you willing that Christ should see the fruit of His death in you? Come to Him, then. Respond to His unparalleled love. Come to the Good Shepherd. He waits to receive you. He has His face to you, and not His back. He has His face to you, and there is not a frown on it; His face beams with compassion and love. Return! O return! to the Shepherd and Bishop of your souls. Return, return, from vanities and idols; return from the ways of disobedience, and sinful pleasure; return from your wanderings in the wilderness of the world; come to the Saviour, and let Him fold you in His arms; come and join yourselves to the Lord in a perpetual covenant that shall not be forgotten.

—Andrew Gray
(1805-1861)
Sermon: *The Seed Corn*
Minister, West Free Church, Perth

ALL THROUGH LIFE I SEE

All through life I see a cross—
    Where sons of God yield up their breath;
There is no gain except by loss;
    There is no life except by death;
    There is no vision but by faith.

—Walter Chalmers Smith
(1824-1908)
The Christian Paradox
Minister, Free High, Edinburgh

WE BEGIN *THERE*

The important thing for us is not the Cross, but the Person Who died on it.... We begin *there*. We are not talking about a heroic man meeting an unfortunate end. If it were only that, there would be no cause for thanksgiving on Good Friday.... But it is far more important to see ourselves as God sees us, because those are the persons we really are, with all the trimmings, pretensions, hypocrisies, and excuses torn aside. And that is what happens to you and me when we have the courage to stand before the Cross. I know then that I am a sinner. I realise that the things that brought Jesus to this are the very things which I hate in myself—the treachery of Judas, the scheming conventionalism of Caiaphas, the compromise of Pilate, the cowardice of the disciples, the callous blindness and indifference of the mob. Self-interest, worldliness, materialism, hatred of the truth—these are the things which crucified the Son of God.

> —Tom Allan
> (1916-1965)
> *The Cross of Calvary*

Preacher, Evangelist

THE HOLY ONE DID HIDE HIS FACE

The Holy One did hide His face;
    O Christ, 'twas hid from Thee!
Dumb darkness wrapt Thy soul a space,
    The darkness due to me;
But now that face of radiant grace
    Shines out in love on me.

> —Anne Ross Cousin
> (1824-1906)
> *Immanuel's Land and Other Poems*

Devotional Poet

DISMEMBERING THE CROSS

What has recognisably happened, if the crudity can be forgiven, is that we have dismembered the Cross. Churchmen carry about the vertical beam, our forgiveness in Christ, and unconsciously escape the turgid demands of its corollary in horizontal obedience.... While the world...carries about the horizontal, forever seeking right relations with neighbour man or neighbour nation, trying to get itself without that Bible knowledge about man's condition that humbles, and about the Christ that alone can totally exalt. Because it is not "engaged" the Faith becomes vacuous. Because it is blind, the world can never glimpse the only way to peace. It is precisely the conjunction of the vertical and the horizontal that, in every case, makes the Cross. And it is the Cross that alone can save.

> —George Fielden Macleod
> (The Lord Macleod of Funiary)
> (1895-   )
> Sermon: *Only One Way Left*

Minister, Founder Iona Community

THE MESSAGE HAD
TO BE AUTHENTICATED

Jesus had said that his Father in heaven was infinitely holy, infinitely loving, infinitely merciful. He had enacted that message in deeds of friendship as impartial and all-embracing as the light and warmth of the sun, leaving behind him a trail of healing and spiritual reinstatement. But to be finally and universally cogent, so that none need feel excluded, too low to be raised, too unlovely to be loved, the message had to be authenticated at the lowest point to which man can fall through their own follies, or be thrust down by the inhumanity of man to man. So at last Jesus hung on a cross....

> —Archibald Campbell Craig
> (1888-   )
> *The Death He Died*

Preacher, Lecturer, Writer

TWO WONDERS I CONFESS

Upon that Cross of Jesus.
    Mine eye at times can see
The very dying form of One
    Who suffered there for me;
And from my smitten heart, with tears,
    Two wonders I confess—
The wonder of His glorious love,
    And my own worthlessness.

> —Elizabeth Cecilia Clephane
> (1830-1869)
> *Breathings on the Border*

Poet

NO ROAD TO EASTER ... EXCEPT—

Did you hear, through this shout of Easter praise and the trumpets of victory, the diapason note of sacrifice? "The God of peace brought again from the dead the Lord Jesus, through the blood of the everlasting covenant." There was no road to Easter for Jesus except by Good Friday; no way to that risen, eternal quality of life except by life laid down. And that being so, this, too, is axiomatic—there is no road to the power of Easter for any of us except at the cost of self-commital; no way to the experience of having God's energies loosed and set free into our life except through the discipline of self-surrender. When all is said and done, the supreme need of the Church...is men on fire for Christ.

> —James Stuart Stewart
> (1896-   )
> *Heralds of God*

Preacher, Theologian, Writer

THE BREATH OF THE RESURRECTION

There can be no real life without breath, movement, growth, and perfection. The breath of the resurrection life is prayer; the movement of the resurrection life is Christian activity; its growth is increase in holiness; and the perfection of the resurrection life is the being made like unto Him when He shall appear the second time with power and great glory.

—James Drummond Burns
(1823-1864)
Fragments
Minister, Hampstead, London

DEATH WAS TRANSFIGURED

He makes death the supreme appeal by which He reconciles His sinful brethren to the Father. Had there been no death, in what language could He have spoken to us of the guilt and folly of sin, and of the love of God, and of the supreme iniquity of sinning against infinite love, of the evil we are cherishing and the good we are resisting? When He rose death for us was not abolished, It was transfigured, and God's holiness and love shone though it, and our highest good, our own supreme strength, shone through it. How except by being made like unto His brethren for the sufferings of death could He have accomplished either this revelation of the Father or the reconciliation of His brethren?

—John Wood Oman
(1860-1939)
Sermon: *The Easter Victory*
Professor of Systematic Theology, Principal, Presbyterian College of England

ONLY THIS WE KNOW

I believe that we shall never clearly understand the true sense of the many dark passages of human affairs till we be on the other side. Only this we know, that though clouds and darkness are round about Him, yet righteousness and judgment are the habitation of His throne, and the inner side of that thick darkness is lined with purest and most perfect light; and how much reason have we to long to see it, and to think this dark night very long, but withal to be relieved with the assurance that the morning is coming, and the day will break, and then all these shadows will flee away.

—Robert Leighton
(1611-1684)
Archbishop of Glasgow; Professor; Minister at Dunblane

WE THINK SO LITTLE OF INVISIBLE WORLD

The chief, if not the only reason, as it seems to me, why our thoughts of the invisible world, and of its great inhabitants, are so faint and shadowy is that we think so little, and to so small purpose, of Him who came out of the realms of the Unseen for us men; and who has for us again returned to the very place to which our friends are being gathered, one after another. The strange reason too comes over us at times that our departed friends, if not destroyed, have yet, in dying, so lost their individuality and their likeness to what they were when with us, as to be incapable of being ever recognised by us again. They seem to have left their humanity and all that is like ourselves, as well as their mortal bodies, in the grave; as if they had vanished into the subtle air, and this keeps our thoughts restrained, and prevents them rising to the invisible.

—John Bruce
(1794-1880)
Sermon
Minister, St. Andrews, Edinburgh

THERE IS NO BREAK

We shall be in eternity what we are making ourselves, or what grace is making us, in time. The same essential nature, and in the same essential state in which our last day on earth left us, we shall carry forward into the other world. Here there is no break, or line of separation between the seen and the unseen state. If, then, you would desire to know what you shall be in regard to all that is most essential in your future being, ask yourselves what you are beginning to be, and are more and more becoming, as the brief space of this momentous spring-tide of our being is passing.

—Islay Burns
(1817-1872)
Sermon: *What We Shall Be!*
Preacher; Professor of Theology, Glasgow

BE GREAT-MINDED LIKE HIM

He came from God; He was going to God. What mattered it what happened to Him, what place He held, what humiliation He endured, in the brief snatch of earthly life between? And we, if we would be great-minded like Him, must have the same high faith, the same heavenly consciousness. We must know that this world, with its wrongs and disappointments, is not all; that this life, with its pride and pomps, is but a passing show. We must remember ever the grander world beyond, the infinite life within, and even now, amid the glare and din of time, live in and for eternity... the consciousness ever glowing in our hearts that we too came from God and are going back to God!

—William Gray Elmslie
(1848-1889)
Sermon: *Our Lord's Treatment
of Erring Friends*
Professor of Hebrew, Presbyterian College, London

April 5

HIS SUN SET IN CLOUDS

Here is one who lived a life of godliness upon earth; but who, from the weakness of his faith, and the imperfection of his graces, could scarcely allow himself to believe that he belonged to the family of God. Fears regarding his eternal condition harassed him through life; and when death came, his hope brightened not into assurance, nor did the luminous prospect beyond the grave open to his view. He passed the gloomy valley without that light and consolation which Christians so generally enjoy. His sun set in clouds. But the stroke is over. Angels waited to convey his separate spirit to Immanuel's happy land, and rapture has succeeded to anxiety and doubt.

—Lady Janet Colquhoun of Luss
(1781-1846)
Out of Great Tribulation

April 6

A FULL LIFE—WHEN GOD IS KNOWN

What a full and pregnant thing life is when God is known; and what a weary emptiness it is without Him!... The river of God is full of water, and He will moisten and fill these parched hearts of ours, out of the river of His own life. Whatever fears, whatever doubts may stir within us, of weariness and withering, let us be ready with our answer: Christ in me, the hope, the eternal hope, of satisfying joy. The untiring state of a spirit is love and duty, and these we have in the Father and the Son. "Thou art my hiding place." "Because I live, ye shall live also!"

—Thomas Erskine of Linlathen
(1788-1870)
Letters
Legal Authority and Theologian

NEITHER YEARS NOR HEARTBEATS

Life is not measured by years or by heart-beats. Life is purpose, effort, experience, feeling, victory. Life is love. Life is self-sacrifice. The life of Christ, of the Christ who came among men, was the very will, and the truth, and the compassion of God working through a human heart and inspiring a human brain.... If the resurrection of Christ and the offer of Christ are of little significance to you, brother, it can only be because you do not want in any true sense to live.... It is the life of God He is offering you—'I will give you the truth, the power, the love that were in Me. Bit by bit, as your capacity for living expands, I will pour all this into you, and you will rise nearer and nearer God, and grow greater in every God-like faculty through eternity, because I live.'

> —John F. Ewing
> (1849-1890)
> *An Easter Sermon*
Minister, Toorak, Melbourne, Australia

LIVE FOR THE FUTURE

God's method is never mere restoration, but enlargement and uplifting and advancement; and He seeks for His fellow-workers men and women who have faith and courage to leave the unreturning past and go forward into the untried future and build a holier Temple in a fairer City. Reverence the past, and read its lessons; but live for the future and believe in the boundless possibilities which it holds for every man who hopes in God and launches out on the ever-advancing, ever-widening stream of His redeeming purpose.

> —David Smith
> (1866-1932)
> Sermon: *The Boundless Possibilities of Grace*
Professor of Theology, Londonderry

LEARNING AND STUDYING

I am, nevertheless, learning and studying, (1) To live by the constant exercise of faith, and not by either carnal or spiritual sense. (2) Constantly to submit to the Lord's will, in crossing mine. (3) To exercise a calm and steady patience under all my trials. (4) To read God's love in my worst evils, desertions, heart-plagues, disappointments, afflictions. (5) To cast out slavish fear, and proud selfishness, out of my heart, and beat in true evangelical principles. (6) To close with Christ more fully, love Him more fervently, walk with Him more closely, and entertain kindly and familiar thoughts of God in Him....(10) To be profitable to others, in the most advantageous Manner. (11) To exercise thankfulness to God for all His mercies, as pledges of heaven, and purchased with the blood of Christ. To make Christ my ALL IN ALL: my wisdom, righteousness, sanctification, and redemption.

> —James Fraser
> (1639-1698)
> *Memoir*

Minister, Culross

OCCUPY TILL I COME

One of the first questions, therefore, which every man who is in the vigour of his age should put to himself is "What am I doing in this world? What have I yet done, whereby I may glorify God, and be useful to my fellows? Do I properly fill up the place which belongs to my rank and station? Will any memorial remain of my having existed on the earth; or are my days passing fruitless away, now when I might be of some importance in the system of human affairs?" Let not any man imagine that he is of no importance, and has, upon that account, a privilege to trifle with his days at pleasure. Talents have been given to all; to some ten, to others five, to others two. *Occupy with these till I come,* is the command of the great Master of all.

> —Hugh Blair
> (1718-1800)
> Sermon: *Middle-aged Men*

Minister, High Kirk, Edinburgh

INSTINCT FOR EXCELLENCE

Love may at first sight seem a doubtful guide. Is it not passionate, blind, and rash? Yet love is after all the only power in all the world that is delicate enough to create the instinct for excellence. That was Jesus Christ's secret long before it was Paul's. He set love free upon the earth, and the effects of that new love which was flooding human life were wonderful indeed to the world, and not less surprising to those into whose heart it had entered. For, in the secret alchemy of God, they found that in their souls love was transmuted into knowledge. Loving much, and knowing themselves greatly loved, they arrived at an accurate and direct sense of the distinction between what was finer and what was poorer.

—John Kelman
(1864-1929)
Sermon: *The More Excellent Way*
Writer; Preacher, Fifth Avenue Presbyterian Church, New York

NOT SOUND IN CREED

What the Church chiefly needs to give her power over the world, is the outworking of the religious principle in the Christian's daily life. I become, as life advances, more impressed with the truth that holy living is the only evidence of a religious state, and that not the sound in creed but the pure in heart shall see God.

—William Landels
(1823-1899)
Preface to a book
Baptist Minister, Regents Park, London

GOSPEL ENJOINS US TO ACTIVATE

Let us ever bear in mind the great and leading doctrines of the faith which we profess, as the foundation of those virtues and graces which the Gospel enjoins us to activate, knowing that the only ground for our acceptance in the sight of heaven is the merits of that blood which flowed from Mount Calvary—and the only evidence we can give that we are washed in this heavenly fountain is by abounding in all manner of holiness and godly conversation. In acknowledging the empire of grace, let us not suppose that we have escaped from under the dominion of reason: but rather let us strive to imitate the prudent and skilful pilot, who, while he fixes his eyes on the needle that points his path through the trackless ocean, quits not the helm that preserves him in his course.

> —James Bryce
> (1785-1866)
> Sermon: *The Pleasantness of Religion*

Chaplain to the Forces, Bengal, India

LIVING THE LIFE THAT TELLS

People think we missionaries go out to these parts of the world, and from morning to night do nothing but preach sermons. It is quite a mistake. It is not the preaching of a sermon so much as the living the life that tells on the native heart. It is by living a divine life, by striving to follow in the footsteps of Him who came to express the Father's love, that we win the heart of the savage, and raise him up to become a true man or woman in Jesus Christ.... The life of holiness is not ease, but encounter; not song, but strife; not ecstasy, but energy; not calmness, but conquest.

> —James Chalmers
> (1841-1901)
> *Letters*

Missionary, New Guinea

I HAVE SIMPLY ALLOWED GOD

I am sometimes asked the secret of my so-called success. I wish I could be conscious of it, but I am not. I have simply allowed God to use my mind and body for His ends, and with His help I have tried to do the root things of life and to leave the secondary things alone.

—James Stewart
(1831-1905)
General Assembly Address, 1900
Missionary, Lovedale, South Africa

OUR WORSHIP COMPELS US

Our worship of the Redeemer compels us to win others for Him. If our worship produces no service, but only a smug selfishness, it is not God the Father we worship, not the Cross of Christ that has been our vision. The Cross is for the whole world, the love of the Father sweeps over the earth; is wider than nationality or race. It is a sea without bank or boundary, and he who looks into the heart of God cannot but say "I must; I cannot forbear; I must live, for the revelation of this message to mankind."

—Donald Fraser
(1870-1933)
Moderatorial Address
Minister; Missionary, Livingstonia, Central Africa

OUTLINE OF THE GOSPEL

That God was the Father of all. That He loved every human soul with a love the measure of which was the agony of His own Son. That He made no choice among His children, selecting some and rejecting others. That His Son came into the world not to win a difficult pardon by shedding His own blood for certain sinners, but to reveal to all God's goodwill towards them and desire to save them by turning them away from their iniquities and to teach them to have a childlike confidence in God: this was the outline of the Gospel which he preached with all the power and persuasiveness of his own living conviction of the truth.

—Robert Hubert Story
(1835-1907)
Funeral Sermon for John McLeod Campbell, 1872

Principal, Glasgow University

ACCOMMODATED TO OUR NATURE

This is the divine process and science of the gospel. The gospel is accommodated to our nature: its light is adapted to our darkness; its mercy to our misery; its pardon to our guilt; its sanctification to our impurity; its comforts to our griefs; and in substituting the love of Christ for the love of sin, in giving us the object to love, it meets our constitution, and, satisfies the strongest cravings of our nature. It engages our affections, and, in taking away an old heart, supplies its place with a new one and a better.

—Thomas Guthrie
(1803-1873)
Sermon: *The New Heart*

Preacher and Philanthropist

HE DISHONOURS GOD

Whoever hears these glad tidings, he dishonours God, he pours contempt of his Saviour's love, and he wrongs his own soul, if he does not receive consolation from them. Be not hindered by what you see in yourselves, unless you are in love with sin, and afraid of being divorced from it. The Gospel is preaching to sinners. It does not expect to find them, but it is intended to make them, holy. A deep and inward sense of your own unworthiness, unless it is prevented by the deceiver, should only make you more highly esteem the grace of the Gospel, and more willingly depend on your Redeemer's love.

—John Witherspoon
(1723-1794)
Sermon: *The Love of Christ
in Redemption*
Minister, Paisley; Principal, Princeton Theological Seminary

THE POWER OF THE RESURRECTION

For this is what Christianity essentially is—a religion of Resurrection. This is what every worshipping congregation is intended in the purpose of God to be—a community of the Resurrection. And this is what the Gospel offers today to this dark and ruined world, where men peering into the future are daunted by the wellnigh impossible task of creating order out of chaos and life out of death—the power of the Resurrection. In short, this is the essential Gospel. Rejoice that the Lord is arisen!

—James Stuart Stewart
(1896-   )
Sermon: *The Power of the
Resurrection*
Preacher, Theologian, Writer

THE FRUIT CALLED FOR

Now there is a fruit called for from these husbandmen. What fruit is this? ye will say. This fruit, sirs, is not such fruit as ye pay your rents with, as corn, hay, or the like, that your hearts love well. Then what fruit is this that is called for? Why, it is faith and repentance, love to God, and obedience to His revealed will, which many of you, yea, the most part of you, are as great strangers to as if ye had never heard the everlasting Gospel preached.

—Alexander Peden
(1626-1686)
The Lord of the Vineyard

Covenanting Preacher

THE TRUE SPECIFIC OF ALL

I am never weary of recurring to the thought of the personal nearness, the mysterious yet most familiar sympathy, the profound and unerring wisdom, the mingled majesty and tenderness of that divine yet gentlest of Consolers. If Christianity had not more than this, this one so beautiful, so real, and wonderfully suitable provision for the deepest yearnings of the heart would be to me proof sufficient of its divine origin. I have all the certainty of moral evidence that this is the true specific for all the unrest and manifold distractions of man's inner life—the peace of God that passeth all understanding, keeping your heart and mind through Christ Jesus.

—John Caird
(1820-1898)

Principal, Glasgow University

HOW HARD IT IS

Oh what need of the powerful presence of the Holy Ghost, without whom a free Saviour will, and must be, a Saviour despised and rejected of men. How hard it is to unite in just proportions the humbling doctrine of man's inability to come to Christ without regeneration, and the free gospel offer which is the moral means employed by God in conversion!

—William Chalmers Burns
(1815-1868)

(On feeling obliged to
defer a candidate for church membership)

SAY, THEN, MY CONSCIENCE

Say, then, my conscience, as thou shalt answer at the judgment-seat of Christ, am I taking this honour of myself, or am I called of God as was Aaron? Is Christ sending me, and laying a necessity upon me to preach the Gospel? While He determines me to follow Providence, and to take no irregular step toward thrusting myself into the office, is He breathing on my soul, and causing me to receive the Holy Ghost? Is He endowing me with tender compassion for the souls of men and with a deep sense of my own unfitness, and earnest desire to be sanctified and be made meet for the Master's use? In the progress of my education, am I going bound in the spirit, with the love of Christ burning in my heart, and constraining me: rendering me willing cheerfully to suffer poverty, contempt, and hatred of all men, for His Name's sake; willing, if possible, to risk my own salvation in winning others to Christ.

—John Brown
(1722-1787)
*Reflections of a Candidate
for the Ministerial Office*

Minister, Haddington

NO DRIFTWOOD FOR GOD!

Men who drift into the ministry, as it is certain so many do, become mere ecclesiastical flotsam and jetsam, incapable of giving carriage to any soul across the waters of life, uncertain of their own arrival anywhere, and of all the waste of their generation, the most patent and disgraceful. God will have no driftwood for His sacrifices, no drift-men for His ministers. Self-consecration is the beginning of His service, and a sense of our own freedom and our own responsibility is an indispensable element in the act of self-consecration.

—George Adam Smith
(1858-1942)
Isaiah

Semitic Scholar; Principal, Aberdeen University

LET YOUR FACE SHINE!

When men seek to entice you to forge communion with God and to follow the world with them, let your face shine with the brightness that comes from your communion with the Master and they will cease to trouble you. Christians can sometimes do more by shining for God than by speaking for Him.

—Andrew A. Bonar
(1810-1899)
Letters
Preacher, Glasgow and Kelso

THE GRACE WHEREIN WE STAND

This inner world of privilege and blessedness and conviction, its citizens the redeemed of all ages, its anointed King holding in thrall the best spirits of each succeeding generation, this Kingdom with its own laws, at once benignant and inexorable, this realm where nothing is bought or sold or earned, but where all is without money and without price, this land of freedom purchased at such a ransom, this high calling whereof we are made ministers, this grace wherein we stand.

—George Johnstone Jeffrey
(1881-1961)
Our Perennial Theme
Minister, Glasgow; Warrack Lecturer

THOSE UNHALLOWED FLAMES OF STRIFE

As for you young gentlemen, especially those that intend theological study, it is my earnest exhortation and advice to you that you avoid as you would the plague that itch for polemical and controversial theology which is so prevalent and infectious, speedily extricate yourselves from those unhallowed flames of strife and controversy, that your minds enlightened by the pure and celestial fire of the divine spirit may shine forth in holiness, and glow with the most fervent charity.

—Robert Leighton
(1611-1684)
Lecture to Students
Archbishop of Glasgow; Professor; Minister at Dunblane

UNTHANKFUL, UNHOLY

Trying today, the anniversary of my first sermon as ordained minister, to review the past and to spend every hour, so far as I have leisure, in prayer for more grace. I am greatly struck with 2 Timothy 3:2: *"unthankful, unholy,"* as characteristics of professing formalists in the last days; but is in another form applicable to myself. Shame and sorrow fill me at my unholiness, after all the kindness of the Lord, opportunities, privileges, seasons of communion, example of other saints, blessings sent. Lord, give, give!

—Andrew A. Bonar
(1810-1899)
Diary, September 23, 1869

Preacher, Glasgow and Kelso

UNSPEAKABLE PLEASURE

What I had experienced in my own soul, was an instantaneous deliverance from all those wrong tempers and affections, which I had long and sensibly groaned under. An entire disengagement from every creature, with an entire devotedness to God; and from that moment, I found an unspeakable pleasure, in doing the will of God in all things. I had also a power to do it, and the constant approbation both of my own conscience and of God.

—Alexander Mather
(1733-1800)
Statement: 1799

Trusted helper of John Wesley

LET ME FIX ON MY SAVIOUR

Let me fix on my Saviour: let my meditation of Him be sweet;
let my soul follow hard after Him in the sweet watches of the
night: and so turn them into the dawn of everlasting day—What
my soul, are all outward enjoyments, but the fancies of a dream,
that will flee away, as soon as conscience, death, or the last
trumpet awaken us?—In our embrace, the earthly visions die:
nothing is worth thy joys, nothing lovely or certain, as thy
God!—How often have I been deluded concerning things of
eternal moment—Oh! to be where there is no night; no
illusions; where endless realities shall fill my whole heart and
mind; where I shall know God Himself, even as, I am known,
and see Him as He is!

—John Brown
(1722-1787)
Of a Harvest Day

Minister, Haddington

YOU HAVE THE SCRIPTURES

You have the Scriptures, search them; since you have
reasonable souls, search them. Other men's faith will not save;
you cannot see to walk to heaven by other men's light, more
than you can see by their eyes. You have eyes of your own,
souls of your own, subordinate to none but the God of spirits,
and the Lord of consciences Jesus Christ; and therefore examine all that is spoken to you from the word and receive no
more upon trust from men, but as you find it upon trial to be
the truth of God.

—Hugh Binning
(1627-1653)
Sermon: *Of the Scriptures*

Minister, Govan, Glasgow

SHALL SHORT SIGHTED CREATURES

Would a criminal, under sentence of death, reject the offers of pardon, life, and liberty, because his gracious sovereign did not think proper to explain to him all the reasons for which he had been pleased to grant him this inestimable favour?...Shall short-sighted ignorant creatures, like man, who are but of yesterday, and thus know nothing, take it upon them to penetrate into all the mysteries of providence, or presume to fathom, by their shallow powers, the deep things of God?

—Alexander Craik
(1772-1856)
Sermon: *1st Timothy 1:15*

Minister, Liberton

THE LIGHT OF LOVE

It is not the presence or absence of intellectual light that is here in question; it is the absence or at least the feebleness of the light of love, the sense of brotherhood. No amount of error discerned in the creed of another, no amount of conscious light in our own hold of what we believe can be any reason for bitterness or even impatience in controversy....It is far more easy to assume an evil in our opponent as explaining what we call his blunders than to do him the justice of trying to reach his standpoint and judge fairly of his error if such it be.

—John McLeod Campbell
(1800-1872)
Reminiscences and Reflections

Minister, Rhu

NARROW BUT NEVER OBSCURE

The story of the Church of God down through the ages is one of *conflict,* but also of *conquest....* Here let me stress one truth: the proof of reality is obedience to the known will of God. It was Christ Himself who declared that entrance to the heavenly kingdom is denied those who merely say, "Lord, Lord," and is awarded only to those who do the will of the Father. The path of His will may be narrow but it is never obscure, as the Lord never leaves us in doubt as to His requirements. But the *Throne Vision,* while it reveals the measure of our responsibility and possibility, also reveals the measure of our resources.

—Duncan Campbell
(1898-1972)
God's Standard

Evangelist

CHURCH AS BODY OF CHRIST

Nowhere is the Church so literally the Body of Christ as when she offers Intercession. No act more closely unites her with her Lord than when, vitalised by His life, instructed by His mind, and guided by His spirit, she pours forth her soul in entreating God's blessing for mankind. She is there indeed the representative of the seeking Saviour. She is there with all the company of the Saints before the Altar of God, offering her own life for the life of the world, that the world may be reconciled to God.

—Oswald B. Milligan
(1879-1940)
The Ministry of Worship

Minister

MAN ON THE MARCH TO GOD

The Christian faith involves the Church. The Christ who reveals the Father, who delivers man, who is alive by His Spirit today, meets us in the community of His people. That community is, looked at from one angle, a struggling, sinning, divided, ineffective institution—not sure how far it is at home in this world. From the other angle it is the divine community, nurse of saints and martyrs, fount of a vast power of healing and teaching, and reconciling ministry, a fellowship of the Spirit, whose head is Christ Himself, in whom and to whom a continuous worship ascends from earth to heaven. It is man on the march to God.

> —David Haxton Carswell Read
> (1910-   )
> *The Christian Faith*
> Minister, Madison Avenue Presbyterian Church, New York

A WORLDLY CHURCH

A worldly Church is the devil's most effective agent for the destruction of immortal souls; a Church of which the members are lovers of pleasure more than lovers of God; a Church in which those who have the form of godliness are denying its power; a Church, the members of which, instead of being living epistles of him who was meek and lowly of heart, of him who said, "Love one another as I have loved you," instead of being distinguished by "righteousness, peace, and joy in the Holy Ghost," are distinguished by all that is most characteristic of the world, pride, covetousness, supreme love of money, and that wrath of man that worketh not the righteousness of God but division and confusion, aversion to spiritual duties, such as prayer and communion with God, and dread of death, from want of heavenly hope.

> —Robert Paisley
> (1808-1879)
> Sermon: *Worldliness: the Sin of*
> *Lost Souls Under the Gospel*
> Minister, St. Ninians

DESPISE NOT ANY OTHER

Keep peace one with another and ever guard the divine gift of charity. Maintain concord with other servants of Christ. Despise not any other of the household of faith who come to you seeking hospitality, but receive and entertain and dismiss them with friendliness and affection, and do not think yourselves better than others of the same faith and manner of life; only with such as err from the unity of Catholic peace have no communion.

—St. Cuthbert
(636-687)
Last Words to the Community

Quoted: Venerable Bede
Vita St. Cuthberti—XXXIX

CHURCH UNITY IN CHRIST

The unity which Jesus Christ would have in His Church is not that of force and constraint but the unity of the Spirit in the bond of peace; it is not like that of a heap of stones thrown together by force, but as lively stones built up into a spiritual house by the cement of love and charity.... But as a living Body animated with a living spirit, speaking the truth in love, receiving all its influences from the Head and growing up into Him in all things.

—Patrick Forbes
(1564-1635)
The Case of the Episcopal Clergy

Bishop of Aberdeen

UNITY IN DIVERSITY

I have been allowed many opportunities of mingling with Christians of other lands, and have learned, I trust, something more of the unity in diversity of the creed, "I believe in the Holy Catholic Church." In that true Church, founded on Christ's sacrifice, and washed in His blood, cheered by its glorious memories and filled with its immortal hopes, I desire to live and die. Life and labour cannot last long with me; but I would seek to work to the end for Christian truth, for Christian missions and for Christian union.

—John Cairns
(1818-1892)
On being presented with his portrait by Lockhart

Preacher, Professor, Principal

PLEASE GOD, REVIVE PRAYER!

O that it would please God to revive among professing Christians a spirit of prayer; and when they cannot unite in sentiment, they may unite in prayer; that when impiety and immorality are bold and insolent, they may oppose them by prayer; and that when they are slandered, insulted, or abused by their enemies, they may find unspeakable comfort in imitating their dying Saviour, loving them that hate them, and praying for them that despitefully use them and persecute them.

—John Witherspoon
(1723-1794)
Sermon: *Fervancy in Prayer*

Minister, Paisley; Principal, Princeton Theological Seminary

WHY FIGHT AGAINST OURSELVES?

Are not all true men that live, or that have ever lived, soldiers of the same army, enlisted under Heaven's captaincy, to do battle against the same enemy—the empire of Darkness and Wrong? Why should we misknow one another, fight not against the enemy but against ourselves, from mere difference of uniform?

—Thomas Carlyle
(1795-1881)
Selected Thoughts

Essayist and Historian

WHO WOULD NOT CHOICE HIM?

Though I had ten thousand times ten thousand years, yea, the faculty of angels, I could in no ways lay out mine obligations to free grace; but behoved, when I had babbled my fill, to seal it all up with this, Christ is matchless.... They that have been most ravished with His love, and most eloquent in the praise of His comeliness, will see that they have been but, at best, babes learning to speak. O what shall I say? He is the most wonderful, glorious, and inestimable Jewel; the incomparable Pearl of price. O, who would not choice Him? who would not give away themselves to Him? Let a man look through heaven and earth, and seek a portion where he will, he shall not find the like of Christ.

—James Renwick
(1662-1688)
Letters
Preacher of the Covenanters and Martyr

TRUST GOD FOR A HUMAN HEART

We may find it difficult to formulate precisely in our own thoughts what is meant by the presence of Christ at God's right hand, and the ministries of His Heavenly Priesthood; but the practical significance is that we can trust God for a human heart as well as for infinite wisdom and power, that we can be assured that we are present to His mind in every detail of our burdens of sorrow and sin, that He understands with the sympathetic understanding of one who knows all the fierceness of our temptations and all the heaviness of our sorrows, and also that the way of the Cross, when appointed by God and followed in trust and submission, is the way to the everlasting crown.

—William Paterson Paterson
(1860-1939)
Sermon: *The Magnetism of the Cross*
Professor of Divinity, Edinburgh

THERE IS NOT...

For Christ is the same today in heaven that He was yesterday when on earth. Consider all that Christ did and suffered—consider all His dealings with all the diversity of characters who presented themselves to Him.... There is not a mourning heart He is not ready to comfort—there is not a drooping spirit that He is not ready to cheer—there is not a returning penitent that He is not ready to pardon—there is not a doubtful soul that He is not ready to confirm—there is not a feeble faith that He is not ready to strengthen. He will not quench the smoking flax nor break the bruised reed.

—David Welsh
(1793-1845)
Sermon: *The Unchangeableness of Christ*

Professor of Divinity, Edinburgh

PRIEST UPON HIS THRONE

O, what strong consolation and good hope, through grace, may the ascension of Christ afford His people! They have a friend in heaven who is possessed of sovereign authority and of infinite compassion. He attends to all their interests, and they are surely safe in His hands. He is a priest upon His throne; and because He ever liveth to make intercession for them, He is able to save them to the uttermost. Whither He is gone they know, and the way they know; and through Him, as the way and the truth and the life, they expect to be brought to the same blessed place where He is, that they may behold His glory. Such a state of mind is heaven begun, or, at any rate, a preparation for heaven. Let us cultivate this heavenly-mindedness. Our conversation is in heaven.

—Robert Buchanan
(1782-1850)
Sermon: *The Ascension of our Saviour*

Minister, Dalkeith

May 18

ACTUALLY UNITED TO GOD

Pentecost was won for us at Calvary; it needed the atonement to make regeneration possible.... Pentecost is a historical proof—a proof in the domain of fact and experience—that sin has been overcome by Christ's death, and that a divine life is again within the reach of men. It is a seal of the great reconciliation; in the possession of the Holy Spirit men are actually united to God in Christ.

> —James Denney
> (1856-1917)
> *Studies in Theology*

Professor of Theology, Glasgow

May 19

ALL THINGS NEW

He comes to you with His Holy Spirit, the Enlightener, so that you will have new eyes for His "unspeakable gift" in Christ; a new wonder at His "exceeding great and precious promises"; and a new certainty that He will keep them always with His Divine faithfulness, on to the end and in the end; a new conviction that "all things work together for good."

> —Adam Wilson Burnet
> (1883-1962)
> Sermon: *Faith Removing Mountains*

Minister, St. Cuthbert's, Edinburgh

May 20

LIFE—LIGHT—STRENGTH

The Holy Spirit, in receiving of the things of Christ and showing them to us, gives us not only spiritual life and light, but also spiritual strength. We need spiritual strength for the right discharge of duty, for the successful resistance of temptation, and the patient and cheerful bearing of trials.

> —George Simmie Smith
> (1822-1899)
> Sermon: *His Holy Spirit*

Minister, Cranstoun

CAPACITY FOR RESPONSE

Christ had to make the soul which should respond to Him and understand Him. He had to create the very capacity for response. And that is where we are compelled to recognise the doctrine of the Holy Spirit as well as the doctrine of the Saviour. We are always told that faith is the gift of God and work of the Holy Spirit.... The death of Christ had not simply to touch like heroism but it had to redeem us into power of feeling its own worth. Christ had to save us from what we were too far gone to feel.

—Peter Taylor Forsyth
(1848-1921)
The Work of Christ
Preacher, Theologian, Writer

DOES GOD DENY HIS SPIRIT?

But to whom does God ever deny a new nature? To whom does He ever refuse His Holy Spirit? To none who earnestly ask for them. Of all His gifts He is most willing to give us the greatest of all, His Holy Spirit. Yes, more willing than to allow His sun to shine upon us or to send us daily bread. The Holy Spirit is a gift which He beseeches all men to ask and receive. If we would resist the world, therefore, successfully; if we would conquer it instead of conforming to it; let us beseech God earnestly and continuously to renew our minds; to give us holy hearts through His Holy Spirit; to do this now, and to be ever doing it, until no elements of the old nature, no principle of 'this world' is to be found in us.

—Robert Flint
(1834-1910)
Nonconformity to this World
Professor of Philosophy, St. Andrews

THE HARVEST WILL FOLLOW

The fruit of the Spirit is the result of His creative power in my life. And if I am to be like Christ in whom these graces were displayed to perfection, then I must first yield myself to the Spirit who was His without measure. Such a surrender will bring the harvest in due season. Let none stumble here through lack of faith. Let none suppose the soil of his heart too unpromising. If weeds will grow there, why not wheat? Even the presence of tares shows that the soil will support life. Look at a seed. It is small, hard, dry, seemingly lifeless. Yet all the possibilities of fragrance, form, taste and colour are there. All the wonder and glory of the life of holiness awaits the full surrender of your forgiven heart to the presence and power of the Holy Spirit. Let the seed be planted. The harvest will follow.

—Frederick L. Coutts
(1899-   )
The Call to Holiness
General of the Salvation Army

UNBELIEF STRUGGLING WITH FAITH

You cannot take fire into your bosom and not be burned. When the Holy Ghost has been taken into your heart, just think of the oppositions and contradictions thenceforth to be found there—unbelief struggling with the faith of God and His salvation, worldliness with the apprehension of the worth of things unseen, coarse ambition with devotion to God's will, selfishness with unselfishness, pride with humbleness of mind, the spirit of the self-reliant man with the spirit of the little child—in one word, sin with its infinite variety, malignity and power with Divine purity and love. The briars and thorns that have overrun human nature will not be burned to the root without pain. It will occasion torture at times. And whosoever thinks this is the language of exaggeration does not know the thing here spoken of.

—Alexander Martin
(1857-1946)
The Baptism of Fire
Preacher; Principal, New College, Edinburgh

INTERPRETED AND VIVIFIED

In every sense of the term the Spirit's work is to testify to Christ—to what He is, to His words, to what He has done and suffered, to what He is to achieve. In this His function, if not His being, as the Spirit of truth is exhausted. And to say that He uses only what is Christ's is not to narrow the range or the means of His action.... All that belongs to the truth of God's Fatherhood is revealed in the Son, and all that is revealed in the Son is interpreted and vivified by the Spirit.

> —James Denney
> (1856-1917)
> *Dictionary of Christ and the Gospels*
Professor of Theology, Glasgow

NOW IN THIS STILLNESS

Now in this stillness, as the breath
　　Of prayer steals upward to the skies,
O give my soul the wings of faith,
　　That it to Thee may gladly rise.
That, breaking through each fleshly link
　　Which binds its being to the clod,
At life's clear wellspring it may drink,
　　Rejoicing in the smile of God.

> —James Drummond Burns
> (1823-1864)
> *Vision of Prophecy and Other Poems*
Minister, Hampstead, London

SPREAD THEM ALL OUT

Come, then, my brothers, with all your wrongs and with all your injuries, real and supposed, great and small; greatly exaggerated and impossible to be exaggerated. And when you stand praying, spread them all out before God. Name them, and describe them to Him. And He will hear you, and He will help you till you are able, under the last and greatest of them, to say, "Father, forgive them: for they know not what they do."

> —Alexander Whyte
> (1837-1921)
> Sermon: *Lord Teach Us to Pray*
Minister, St. George's, Edinburgh

PONDER BEFORE PRAYING

A Christian before he go to prayer, should study to have a deep impression of those things which he is to make the matter of his supplication to God, and to have them engraven upon his heart.... Oftentimes we speak many things with our lips, ere we study to have our hearts inditing these things that we speak. It were no doubt the great advantage of the Christian in the exercise of prayer, to be much taken up in the obedience of this command, Ecclesiastes 5:2, *Be not rash with thy mouth, and let not thy heart be hasty to utter anything before God; for God is in heaven, and thou upon the earth, therefore let thy words be few....* O that our hearts might speak more in prayer, and our tongues less.

—Andrew Gray
(1630-1652)
Sermon: *To the Duty of Prayer*

Minister, Glasgow

PRAY FOR CLEAR VIEWS

You can do nothing aright without prayer. It is the channel by which spiritual blessings can alone be obtained. Your spiritual enemies are constantly striving to interrupt your impartial self-examination. You cannot in your own strength resist them: therefore pray. Pray for clear views of the nature of faith, and for clear views of the character of that faith which you really have. Pray for the help of the Holy Spirit to strengthen your weak efforts, to humble your natural vanity, and to enable you to appreciate the value of spiritual things. If you thus examine yourselves, conscientiously, scripturally, and prayerfully, you will see your weaknesses and your wants.

—Robert Wodrow Thomson
(1819-1877)
Sermon: *On Self-Examination*

Minister, Ormiston

SO—LET US PRAY

As the earthly father with patient and comprehending love listens to his little child, helps it out when its words fail, watches its face, pieces together its lispings and stammerings—so with completer insight and more perfect tenderness does the Intercessor help us out, and in the end gives us desires as well as words. So out of the seething darkness, out of the stinging conscience, out of the formless horrors, out of the black despair—let us pray.

—William Robertson Nicoll
(1851-1923)
That Unbelief Is the Sin of Sins
Preacher, Publisher, Writer

HE KNOWS HOW TO GIVE

Fear not, then, that any thing really requisite for your support and encouragement in that way shall be withheld. Your Saviour died that you might live; and He continually intercedes with acceptance for all who follow His steps. Has God given you Jesus Christ, and with Him shall He not also give you all good? He knows how to give the Holy Spirit unto them that ask Him. Ask and you shall receive. At every step of your progress remember who has said it, let your dependence be on its truth, and your prayer be for its accomplishment.

—John Gilchrist
(1771-1849)
Sermon: *Matthew 7:13-14*
Minister, Canongate, Edinburgh

FIRST ESSENTIAL OF TRUE PRAYER

Desire is indeed the first essential of true prayer, and desire is a strenuous emotion; it is not a mere wish. Desire, according to the Psalmists, is "thirst," "panting," "longing"; and without the initial discipline of a fervent desire nothing can be understood of the life of prayer as they understood it. Let us remember also that their desire was after God Himself, not His gifts; not even forgiveness and salvation, save as these came with Himself. But desire is only an emotion at its best, of itself most impotent. It must, as soon as it is consciously present, be followed up by determined steadfast action of the will. "Seeking" and "Searching" follow "Longing." Of some few it may indeed be true, "I am found of Him that sought not for me"; but the normal wholesome way into the presence of God is, as we have seen, a desire which is a demand, and a quest. "O Lord, Thou art my God: earnestly do I seek Thee."—Psalm 53:1.

—Annie H. Small
(1857-1945)
Missionary to India; Principal, St. Colms, Edinburgh

WE PRAY BECAUSE...

We pray to God because we believe He is able and willing to help us, and because we hope in His sacred promises, and through the merits of Christ that He will help us. Prayer is therefore an act of religion, because by it we acknowledge our weakness, misery, and unworthiness, our dependence upon God, and our subjection to Him; and also by it we confess Him to be our sovereign Lord, and the giver of all good, and we honour His infinite goodness, from which we hope to obtain what we stand in need of. It is also, like all other good things, a gift of God, for of ourselves we are not "sufficient to think a good thought."

—George Hay
(1729-1811)
Prayer
Roman Catholic Bishop of Edinburgh

MOST COURAGEOUS PRAYER ON EARTH

Do you not see how great an achievement it is to be able to say sincerely, "Amen. Even so, come, Lord Jesus"—come as Thou hast always come, with a sword, with increase of truth which will compel us to change our poor scheme of doctrine, with increase of righteousness which will free us to break up our unrighteous ways of life? It is a great prayer and demands a great courage. The man who can pray it honestly has no need to wait for some dim and distant day of judgment at the end of the ages: every day is judgment day, and every day he stands before the Son of Man.

—John Smyth Carroll
(1853-1923)
The Most Courageous Prayer
Minister, St. John's, Glasgow

A TWO-FOLD FIRE

Of old the Lord used to answer His people's prayers and sacrifices by fire from heaven: pray that He may answer yours in like manner, by kindling a holy fire in your soul, as He did in the hearts of the two disciples going to Emmaus; even a two-fold fire, to wit, a *fire of love to Christ,* and a *fire of indignation* against sin. O love the Lord Jesus Christ as your Treasure and Portion; let your thoughts be mainly upon Him, and your soul's breathings after Him. Be much concerned for His interest and Cause, and for the spreading of His kingdom and glory in the world. And be looking out, and longing for the full and perfect enjoyment of Him.

—John Willison
(1680-1754)
The Communicant's Errand
Minister at Dundee

PRAYER "IN THE SPIRIT"

Paul speaks of prayer "in the Spirit," by which, I believe, he meant prayer that was intimate, reverent, passionate, continuing and, above all, expectant. There is no more inspiring example of such prayer than the prayer with which he closes the third chapter of his Letter to the Ephesians. It is prayer addressed to the Father, as are the characteristic Christian prayers. It is prayer that seeks the indwelling of Christ through the agency of the Spirit.

—Charles Sim Duthie
(1911-   )
God in His World
Principal of New College, University of London

LET US INQUIRE

In asking corporal things, let us first inquire if we be at peace with God in our conscience by Jesus Christ, firmly believing our sins to be remitted in His blood? Secondly, let us inquire of our own hearts, if we know temporal or substance not to come to man by accident, fortune, nor chance, neither yet by the industry and diligence of man's labour; but by the liberal gift of God only, whereof we ought to laud and praise His wisdom, goodness, and providence alone. If this be truly acknowledged and confessed, let us boldly ask of him whatever is necessary for us, as sustentation of this body; health thereof; defence from misery; deliverance from trouble; tranquility and peace to our common weal, prosperous success in our vocations, labours, and affairs, whatever they be. And also by asking and receiving these corporal commodities, we have taste of his sweetness and be inflamed with his love, that thereby our faith of reconciliation and remission of our sins may be exercised and take increase.

—John Knox
(1505-1572)
*The True Nature and
Object of Prayer*
Reformer; Minister at St. Giles, Edinburgh

PRAYING IN THE HOLY SPIRIT

Prayer is the atmosphere of revelation, in the strict and central sense of that word. It is the climate in which God's manifestation bursts open into inspiration.... Prayer is the secret of creation, its destiny, that to which it all travails. Before we give even our prayer we must first receive. The Answerer provides the prayer.... What we offer is drawn from us by what God offers... the spirit of prayer flows from the gift of the Holy Ghost, the great Intercessor.... In Christ's intercession our best prayer, broken, soiled, and feeble as it is, is caught up and made prayer indeed, and power with God.... This is praying in the Holy Ghost, which is not necessarily a matter either of intensity or elation. This is praying "for Christ's sake." If it be true that the whole Trinity is in the Gospel of our salvation, it is also true that all theology lies hidden in the prayer which is our chief answer to the Gospel.

—Peter Taylor Forsyth
(1848-1921)
Preacher, Theologian, Writer

KEEP AN AMPLE MARGIN

But experience and need, even when taken together, do not exhaust the fulness of God, and we must call in faith to guide us in our prayers, for He is able to do exceeding abundantly above all that we ask or think. There is room in Christ for wide expansions, and therefore in thought and prayer we must always keep an ample margin.... There are duties unattempted, promises unexplored, comforts unimagined, victories undreamed of, and thus, in its form, the redemptive Name is left vague and uncompleted. That He will be is declared, but what will be is unexpressed. In good days and in evil, in work and in weakness, in prosperity and in fear, He will yet more fully declare Himself. For He, the Lord, has said, "I will not leave you comfortless, I will come to you."

—William Malcolm Macgregor
(1861-1944)
Sermon: *The God to Whom We Pray*
Professor, New Testament, Glasgow

BY TELLING GOD ... WE CAN LEARN

If we are dealing with a government department there may be nothing for it but to apply on the printed form and sign on the dotted line; but if we are dealing with a father we may exercise more freedom of speech. Prayer is the means of establishing agreement between God's will and men's desires: and it may well be that the best of all ways of educating our desires is to express them to God in prayer. It may be that it is only by telling God frankly what we want that we can learn what we truly need.

—Thomas Walter Manson
(1893-1958)
The Sayings of Jesus
Professor of Biblical Criticism and Exegesis, Manchester

PRAYER IS A GOOD DESIRE

Prayer is the expression of a good desire. The human heart is full of restless desires, and the prayers of men consist for the most part of the unsifted petitions which are urged by their varying passions. To desire what is right, and to desire it consistently, and passionately, is the first condition of true living; the desires can be corrected only by truth, the mind must apprehend God, and then it will say 'There is none upon earth that I desire beside Thee.'

George Macdonald
(1824-1905)
Unspoken Sermons

Minister, Writer, Poet

LORD, TEACH US TO PRAY!

Prayer is the soul's sincere desire,
    Uttered or unexpressed;
The motion of a hidden fire,
    That trembles in the breast.

O Thou by whom we come to God—
    The Life, the Truth, the Way!
The path of prayer Thyself hast trod;
    Lord, teach us how to pray!

               —James Montgomery
                (1771-1854)
Moravian Minister; Poet; Missionary, West Indies

THEY COULD NOT HEAL US

Where are they who will truthfully go to him in confiding prayer, saying,—"Lord Jesus, we have tried many Physicians, and they could not heal us; now we go to thee:—we are dead in trespasses and sins, poor and needy, blind and naked. The harvest is past, and the summer ended; yet we, guilty sinners, are not saved. But we are spared—and we have heard the glad tidings that there is balm in Gilead—and that thou art the Physician there—able and willing to save to the uttermost all who go to thee. Our hope is in thy Word. We believe; help our unbelief. We give ourselves, soul, spirit, and body, into thy hands. Send us adversity or prosperity, life or death. Give to us what remedies seem to thy love and wisdom best suited to us, and humble hearts to receive them; but, for thy great mercy, save our poor perishing souls!"

               —Norman MacLeod
                (1812-1872)
                Sermon: *The Disease and the Remedy*

Minister, Dalkeith

FROM AN EVIL HEART OF UNBELIEF

From an evil heart of unbelief, from superstition, from incredulity, from rash intrusion where I should not inquire, and from careless or superstitional acquiescence where I should inquire: Good Lord, deliver me.

—Lady Blanche Balfour
(1825-1872)

THOU HAST DRAWN OUT

O Loving, gracious, and bountiful Father! I render all praise unto Thee, for Thy manifold mercies showered on me Thy poor servant: which are more in number than I can recount. Behold, Thou hast not taken me away in my sin, but has spared me long and at last has given me a sight of my sins, a lively sorrow in my heart for the same, a fervent desire to abstain from doing evil, and to do that which is pleasant in Thy sight.... Thou hast let me know mine own weakness and unworthiness, and Thy justice and mercy: Thou hast drawn me unto Thee, as it were, by force and would not suffer me to persevere in wickedness.... Thou hast drawn out fervent prayers, sighs, and sobs from my heart, and tears from mine eyes, for my sin, which I could never have done of my self, without the motion of Thy Holy Spirit.

—Alexander Hume
(*c.*1557-1609)
Prayer of Deliverance from
Vexation of the Spirit

Poet, Minister at Logie

I KNOW GOD ANSWERS PRAYER

My life is one long, daily, hourly record of answered prayer.
For physical health, for mental overstrain, for guidance given
marvellously, for errors and dangers averted, for enmity to the
Gospel subdued, for food provided at the exact hour needed,
for everything that goes to make up life and my poor service, I
can testify, with a full and often wonder-stricken awe, that I
know God answers prayer.

> —Mary Mitchell Slessor
> (1848-1915)
> *Letters*

Missionary to Nigeria

THE WORST SIN

The worst sin is prayerlessness. Overt sin, or crime, or the
glaring inconsistencies which often surprise us in Christian
people, are the effect of this, or its punishment....Not to want
to pray, then, is the sin behind sin; and it ends in not being able
to pray. That is its punishment—spiritual dumbness, or at least
aphasia, and starvation.

> —Peter Taylor Forsyth
> (1848-1921)
> *The Soul of Prayer*

Preacher, Theologian, Writer

SUCH ARE THE PRAYERLESS

Who neglect and lay aside this daily duty of prayer, renounce all communion with God, and say they are content to live in the world without God, and without Christ; without all fellowship with the Father, and with His Son, Jesus Christ. O! what an honour and honourable advantage are they satisfied to live without a communion with God? What a miserable case we would judge that man to be in, who had not one bosom friend in all the world, unto whom he might open all his heart, and make known all his mind. But how much more case must he be in, who hath not God as his near friend, Yea, who deliberately and wilfully refuseth fellowship with God, and will not keep up correspondence with him, and open his heart before him, and make all his desires known unto him. Now such are they, who lay aside prayer, and will not call upon God.

—John Brown of Wamphray
(1610-1679)
Neglect of Prayer
Minister, Scotch Church, Rotterdam, Holland

IN OUR OWN EXPERIENCE

Brethren, we can read not only in Scripture, but in our own experience that man cannot live by bread alone, but by every word which proceedeth out of the mouth of God.

—Adam of Dryburgh
(*c.* 1140-*c.* 1212)
Ad Viros Religiosos

EVERY CONNECTION OF LIFE

The book of Psalms beyond every book of man, and most part of the Book of God can be brought into every connection of life. We can take passage after passage, and write out for it some grief it has comforted, some doubt it has solved, some deliverance it has wrought or celebrated, some hope it has fulfilled. There are promises in the Bible which seem beyond our reach, we have nothing to draw with, and the well is deep. But Someone like ourselves has been before us, and has left a cup to be let down with His Name and story engraven on the rim "For this shall every one that is godly pray unto Thee, in a time when Thou mayest be found."

—John Ker
(1819-1886)
Sermons
Minister, United Presbyterian, Glasgow

THE FRIVOLOUS MAY FEEL

Experience, history and science all concur with the Word of God in the view which they present of the state of things in which they are placed. The vain and frivolous may feel as if the Scriptures have drawn too dark a picture of our world, when they describe it as a scene of sin and suffering, with terrible conflicts within and without. But all who have had large experience of human life will be ready to acknowledge that the account is a correct one. The faithful representation of human character is to many the most satisfactory evidence of the truthfulness of the Word of God.

—James McCosh
(1811-1894)
Sermon: *Unity With Diversity*
President, Princeton Theological Seminary

TO LIFT THE LATCH

Within this sacred Volume lies
The mystery of mysteries!
Happiest they of human race
To whom our Lord has granted grace
To read, to fear, to hope, to pray;
To lift the latch and find the way;
And better had they ne'er been born
Who read to doubt or read to scorn.

—Sir Walter Scott
(1771-1832)
The Monastery

Lawyer, Author, Poet

THE HAPPIEST THING IN LITERATURE

The New Testament.... The happiest thing in literature, with the sound of singing in it everywhere, opening with the choir of angels over Bethlehem and closing with the Hallelujah Chorus of the redeemed.

—Arthur John Gossip
(1873-1954)
Preacher and Professor, Trinity College, Glasgow

WHEN WE HEAR AND ANSWER

None of us is born a Christian. We are born with certain Christian advantages, and certain Christian associations, but every generation has got to be born anew. How will it take place? We become Christian when we hear and accept that Word which at the same time is so simple and winsome and kind, and so awful and imperious and challenging—The Word of God. And when we hear and answer that infallible Word of God, which never led men astray, then we are born again.

—George Sinclair Gunn
(1900-1961)
Sermon: *God's Word*
Minister, Broughton Place, Edinburgh

TREAT IT AS AN APOSTLE

Christ did not come to bring a Bible but to bring a Gospel. The Bible arose afterwards from the Gospel to serve the Gospel. We do not treat the Bible aright, we do not treat it with the respect it asks for itself, when we treat it as a theologian, but only when we treat it as an apostle, as a preacher, as the preacher in the perpetual pulpit of the Church.... The Bible, the preacher, and the Church are all made by the same thing—the Gospel.

—Peter Taylor Forsyth
(1848-1921)
*Positive Preaching and the
Modern Mind*
Preacher, Theologian, Writer

THE FOOD OF THE SOUL

Truth is the food of the soul. The truths of divine revelation are the means of producing, nourishing, and increasing the spiritual life. God works on men in a way suited to their rational natures, and to the established connection between the understanding and the will. He begins with enlightening the understanding, that the light and force of truth may sweetly attract the will to a right choice. Thus in *God's light,* the believer *sees light,* so that God's mind and will revealed in the Scriptures become his also. Where this heavenly lamp points out the way, he cheerfully follows.

—John Erskine
(1721-1803)
Nature of Christian Faith
Minister, New Greyfriars, Edinburgh

WHEN DISSATISFIED

When dissatisfied and bewildered among human illustrations of the truth, I think it is a good escape for the mind to look at the truth as it is in the Bible—to sit down to it just as if I were reading it for the first time, with the conscious ignorance and docility of a child—to stir myself there that I may hold of God, and lay hold of Christ, just as God hath set Him forth to me.

—Thomas Chalmers
(1780-1847)
Correspondence
Mathematician, Preacher, Leader

99

THIS CURIOUSLY FASHIONED BOOK

Men and women, suddenly grown conscious of the shortness of their life and of the extremity of their spiritual need have...picked up this curiously fashioned Book, have marvelled at its interesting structure and its exhaustless beauty, perchance have toyed with it, idly musing. But when, moved by some impulse they know not whence, they have set the ear of their spirit to it, there bursts upon their soul the solemn Voice of Eternity, deep calling unto deep within. Happy are such who, hearing, bow their head and in their hearts make answer: 'Father, Eternal, we hear Thy call. We understand. Help us to keep Thy word and to do Thy will.'

—William Alexander Curtis
(1876-1961)
Sermon: *The English Bible*
Professor of Biblical Criticism, Edinburgh

I SEE SOMETHING HIGHER

The Bible is, indeed, simple enough for the simple, but it is also unfathomably deep. No book takes such an entire sweep of all that affects and interests man....No book begins so low or ends so high. The most tainted being, whose face is one plague-spot from brow to chin, gets a new knowledge of himself here, not with the contaminating knowledge of curiosity but with the healing and hallowing knowledge of repentance. And the most holy saint, the face that seems to its fellows already radiant with the beatific vision, looks in and says, "Hush! for I see something higher, holier still."

—Robert William Barbour
(1854-1891)
Thoughts
Minister, Cults, Aberdeenshire

STUDY NOT MADE IN VAIN

Almighty and most merciful God, Who has given the Bible to
be the revelation of Thy great love to man, and of Thy power
and will to save him: grant that our study of it may not be made
in vain by the callousness or carelessness of our hearts, but that
by it we may be led to repentence for our sins, filled with hope,
made strong for service; and above all filled with the true
knowledge of Thee and of Jesus Christ our Lord.

—George Adam Smith
(1858-1942)
Prayer (adapted)
Semitic Scholar; Principal, Aberdeen University

BEFORE YOU GO TO BED

Now I have just one request to make, and that is that every one
of you this night, before you go to bed, read a portion of this
Bible; and to prevent loss of time, and any excuse for not
complying with the request, I specify the third chapter of the
Gospel of John as that which I want you to read; and then in the
faith of what that chapter contains, fall down on your knees and
pray the God who is the author of the Bible, for the sake of His
Son, and by the operation of His good Spirit, to teach and
enable you so to use your Bible as that you may not "perish but
have the everlasting life" which is in it. Such a prayer, if
sincerely offered, will certainly be heard.

—John Brown
(1784-1858)
Sermon: *The Bible*
Minister, Broughton Place, Edinburgh

BY GOD WE BELIEVE

By God we believe all things in heaven and earth, visible and invisible, to be retained in their being, and to be ruled and guided by His inscrutable Providence, to such end as He has appointed them.

—Scots Confession
1560

HE GIVES GRACE AND GLORY

What is God? He is *Sun and Shield*. Light when I am in darkness, Bulwark when I am outclassed and threatened by my adversaries. What does He bestow? He *will give grace and glory,* redemption in its initiation and redemption in its coronation, morning and noonday, first-fruits and harvest home. It is a pregnant language, and the New Testament is its commentary. God is the Author of Grace: for He sends Christ to provide it through blood and death, and the Holy Spirit to convey it in actual possession to our separate souls. He is Architect of glory; fitting heaven for us through Christ, and through the Holy Spirit fitting us for heaven. All to Him we owe; yet we have our part—to receive His supply, to leave ourselves in His keeping, and to go rejoicing on our way; a simple part, but an essential one.

—Alexander Smellie
(1857-1923)
Sermon: *The Well by the Way*
Minister, Original Secession, Carluke

A MUTUAL INDWELLING

Communion with God is often described as a mutual indwelling; without faith we cannot enter into His heart; without obedience He cannot enter into ours. To have a completed circle of communication, both must be united. With the removal of the obstruction on either side, there comes the free circulation of life.

—Robert Smith
(1816-1894)
Sermon
Minister of Corsock

YOU ARE DIFFERENT

The last word in this world is not sin but grace, not disease but healing, not death but life, not man but God. Forgiveness with God is not a mere sentiment, but a cleansing energy, a restoring force. If you have honestly repented you know that that hideous self which rises up before you to disturb your peace is not your present self at all. *You* are different. That old self is dead, buried, covered up out of sight in that "plenteous grace to cover all our sin." It is true that you have to begin at the very beginning, go on step by step; but can you not believe that the cleansing and renewing is at work in and beneath and around all your endeavours, and that for every stone of a new life that you lay, God lays two. Yes, the incredible thing happens. God makes the defiled life clean again.

—James Gilchrist Goold
(1867-1923)
Divine Renewals
Minister, North Morningside

REMOVE THE CROSS!

How is the Father known? Remove the Cross, and how are God and man brought into harmony, reconciled? Remove the Cross, and where is the goal at once and the grand starting-point to the Imitation of Christ? Remove the Cross, and where is the very nerve and nexus of the new membership? Remove the Cross, and where is the promise of perfected salvation?

—Robert William Barbour
(1854-1891)
Thoughts
Minister, Cults, Aberdeenshire

THE ETERNAL FAVOURS

The heavens declare God's glory, and the firmament his handi-work, and we are inexcusable for not taking more pains to contemplate God's perfections in them—his Almighty power, and incomprehensible wisdom, and particularly his infinite goodness. But the effects of the divine goodness in the works of creation are only temporal favours: the favours purchased to us by the cross of Christ are eternal.

—John Maclaurin
(1693-1754)
Sermon: *Glorying in the
Cross of Christ*

Minister, Glasgow

BOUND TO ARISE

Troubled soul, thou art not bound to feel but thou art bound to arise. God loves thee whether thou feelest or not. Thou canst not love when thou wilt, but thou art bound to fight the hatred in thee to the last. Try not to feel good when thou art not good, but cry to Him who is good. He changes not because thou changest. Nay, He has an especial tenderness of love toward thee for that thou art in the dark and hast no light, and His heart is glad when thou dost arise and say, "I will go to my Father.".. . Fold the arms of thy faith, and wait in the quiet-ness until light goes up in thy darkness.

—George Macdonald
(1824-1905)
The Eloi

Minister, Writer, Poet

A HOME BECAUSE...

The Gospel would be no Gospel at all unless it flung its beam right across the black, gaping gulf of death, and lit up enough of the new world concealed there to show that it is a home. Yes, a *home:* because dwelt in and pervaded by God. There is always a home where there is a father.... Are we not mysteriously unwilling, in spite of all that we know of Christ, to believe that God is love and that He is our Father?

—Hugh Ross Mackintosh
(1870-1936)
Sermon: *Not Bondmen But Sons*
Professor of Systematic Theology, Edinburgh

SOLVING WORD FOR THIS UNIVERSE

All our questions fall back upon deeper questions, and those on deeper still, until they pause before the Great and Awful question as to what this life of ours may mean. Are we human beings irrelevant to this vast system which was our cradle and become our grave? Or is there a blessed hypothesis which thinking, feeling man can honourably hold—a hypothesis which without robbing life of its mystery and awe ends for us its aching ambiguity. May we speak to man of God? There is one solving word for this universe: it is God. There is one solving word for God: it is Christ.

—John Alexander Hutton
(1868-1947)
Warrack Lectures 1921
Preacher; Editor, *British Weekly*

TOO HIGH FOR GRACE

Every man tries to make a bargain with his Maker, and thinks that his Maker desires to make a bargain with him; he conceives of the great Redeemer as seeking to get as much as He can, and he tries to get as much as he can out of the divine Saviour; for all men are deeply mercenary in their hearts. So men refuse grace, refuse that which alone can save them not because they are too low for it, but because they are too high. We are too sunk, too lost, for anything but grace, But oh, the grace is sufficient though nothing else is.

—Alexander Moody Stuart
(1809-1898)
Sermon: *The Manifold
Sufficiency of Grace*

Minister, St. Luke's, Edinburgh

HISTORY WRITES LARGE

And if there is any lesson history has written large across our times, it is this: We live in a universe that is morally on the square and whenever this fact is flouted or ignored, there follows a violent shaking of human destiny, during which little people cry out in despair, while men and women of faith declare: "The Lord God omnipotent reigneth!"

—Donald MacLeod
(1913-   )
Sermon: *The Unshaken Kingdom*

Professor, Princeton Theological Seminary

THERE IS SUCH A THING

It is very true that the longer one lives and learns, the less one is inclined to lay down rules for God as to the way in which He brings men to Himself and the steps by which He does it; or as to the measure of light and the form of thought and feeling under which His children may be holding communion with Him. Thank God, all our thoughts about this are nothing to the various and unsearchable grace of His ways. But we must be born again; there is such a thing as becoming conscious of the call of Christ as something for ourselves; there is such a thing as submitting to the righteousness of God; there is such a thing as a contrite heart being persuaded of the lovingkindness of the Lord; there is such a thing as receiving power to become a son of God.

> —Robert Rainy
> (1826-1906)
> Sermon: *Characteristics and Teaching of Wesley*

Principal, New College, Edinburgh

GOD'S EVOKING

He has spoken to you in sharp rebukes of conscience, and in your secret loathings of the sins you have committed. The noble and generous emotions, and the tender and gracious memories, by which you have, from time to time, been thrilled, were of His evoking. The appreciations of goodness, and the aspirations after purity and holiness, which swept through your soul, were called forth by Him. The longings and ambitions, by which you have once and again been urged, to have your life made great and serviceable in behalf of righteousness and the welfare of your fellows, were kindled by His words. The solemn and overwhelming thoughts of God, which loomed up in your mind and marked an epoch in your history, were communicated to you by His presence. He has been addressing you since the days of your infancy and childhood. He is seeking to be recognised by you.

> —Alexander Beith Macaulay
> (1871-1950)
> Sermon: *The Unrecognised Christ*

Professor of Apologetics, Glasgow

UNDER THE MICROSCOPE

The Eternal One is not a natural object on which we can focus
our telescopes or microscopes. In a question with Him it is we
who are under the microscope.

—Sir Thomas Murray Taylor
(1897-1962)
Sermon: *Walking by Faith*
Professor of Law; Principal, Aberdeen University

THE ONE THING NEEDFUL IS LACKING

Without the oil of the Spirit, our lamps have no light. We may
be regular and conscientious in our stated prayers, diligent in
our attendance at Church, in our use of the means of grace. We
may be students of the Scriptures, or constant readers of
theological books, or experts in theological discussions. We
may be intensely interested in Church affairs. We may be
excellent organisers, and full of energy in all sorts of good
works. We may be very Martha's in our religious activities. But
the one thing needful is lacking—the reality of personal
spiritual life, in which, withdrawn from every external, we
are "acquainted with God," and are conscious of a personal
relationship as real and intimate as that which binds us to a
friend.

Cosmo Gordon Lang
(1864-1945)
Archbishop of Canterbury

SUCH KNOWLEDGE IS IGNORANCE

There is a false knowledge by which God is known as the dread and infinite Being, dwelling in mysterious glory far away in the clouds, possessed of marvellous attributes, which we discuss and analyse and arrange in logical order, but having no more vital connection with our hearts and souls than the lifeless corpse with the anatomist who dissects it. Such knowledge is but ignorance of God. What the knowledge of the moral law is to the spiritual man, what the forms of beauty are to the genius, that the knowledge of God is to the devout mind....God is love; and when we learn to know that love in all its depth and intensity, when we recognise its massive proportions in the guidance of the world's history, and feel its all-embracing tenderness in every episode of our own lives, we cannot but render back to God the love He has lavished on us.

> —Adam Semple
> (1844-1914)
> Sermon: *Eternal Life*

Minister, Huntly

I CANNA DOUBT THE END

How great the gain, the strength, the peace, if you can say this day with assured conviction, say it in the face of every experience, through light and darkness, in life and death, "I believe in God." True, not only in the individual life but in the larger life of the nations, "God is, and God reigns." "God's hand is on the helm of the universe," and with my friend of the hills (an old Highland shepherd) I add: "I canna doubt the end, for God was at the beginning."

> —Ronald G. Macintyre
> (1863-1954)
> Sermon: *In the Beginning God*

Professor of Theology, Sydney, Australia

THIS NON-RELIGIOUS MAN

There are many in the land today, and within the church, who hesitate to call themselves Christians because, as they confess, they have not what they judge to be a right mind towards God. It is not that they deny God: it is that they do not know God, and that they do not love God. They cannot love one they do not know, and God is to them simply the intelligence in the universe and the principle of life. They have nothing to do with Him, and He has nothing to do with them, and therefore, they would not call themselves religious. And yet this non-religious man, who has no profession of faith, and accounts himself unworthy to approach the Sacrament, may be the most loyal of husbands and the most self-sacrificing of fathers, as well as a charitable citizen and a reliable friend. He did it all to his fellow-men, my friend says, which shows some lack of imagination. But God...claims every act is done as done to Him. He has not known God, so my friend says, which is a serious loss of comfort. But there is something more important and decisive— God has known him, God is loving him, and in a day to come God is going to reward him.

—John Watson
(1850-1907)
Sermon: *The Inspiration of Our Faith*

Pastor and Professor

GOD WHO CALLS—SUSTAINS

Those who have been led to feel in some solemn hour that the hand of God has shaped their past and that the voice of God is calling them, may go forward with quiet and fearless hearts to the work that is theirs to do, strong in the assurance that the God who has called them will also sustain them. In no conflict or crisis will they ever be alone, but evermore they will be beset behind and before by the most high God.

—John Edgar McFadyen
(1870-1930)
Sermon: *Predestination*

Professor of Old Testament, Glasgow

SETTING THE LORD BEFORE US

In the universal proneness of the human race to forget God, and to let His glory pass unnoticed, we may see one of the strongest evidences and most degrading effects of our original and universal corruption. And the same considerations exhibit the importance of *setting the Lord always before us;* that by preserving the impressions of His continual presence with us, we may habitually bear in mind our obligations to seek His glory.

—John Martin
(1787-1837)
Tract: *On the Glory of God*

Minister, Kirkcaldy

WE BLESS THEE ... WE BELIEVE

O God, eternal and invisible, we bless Thee that we have seen Thy glory in Jesus Christ. We believe that He came out from Thee, that no soul of all Thy children might cry in vain for the vision of Thy face. We believe that in His life and character He made Thee known. We believe that in His sympathy with men He revealed Thine infinite compassion for our sinful race. We believe that on His Cross we behold Thy redeeming mercy and grace. We adore Thy love revealed in Jesus Christ. Redeem us into a life of love.

—John Hunter
(1849-1917)
Devotional Services
Congregational Minister and Devotionalist, Trinity, Glasgow

THE KEEPING OF GOD

The keeping of God is an omnipotent keeping. I want to get linked with the Omnipotent One. Why is it that we, the children of Pentecost know so little of what it is to walk step by step with Almighty God? I can experience the power and goodness of God only so far as I am in fellowship with Him. Omnipotence was needed to create the smallest thing, and Omnipotence is needed to keep the smallest thing. You must learn to know and trust Omnipotence. A godly life is a life full of God. This keeping is continuous and unbroken. All life is an unbroken continuity, and the life of God is His Almighty power working in us. *Let us make Omnipotence the measure of our expectation.*

> —Andrew Murray
> (1828-1917)
> Address: Regent Square Church,
> London, 1895

Minister and Devotional Writer, South Africa

HOUR WHEN HE WAS CLOSEST

Is there a Providence so individual as that? Is there a divine knowledge extending even to the greatness of my solitude, to the uttermost loneliness of that walk through which I seem to travel in the valley of death's shadow? That was of all others the time when I thought myself to be walking alone—my God seemed to have passed by on the other side, and yet at the same time it was all known. I can see that the hour when I seemed to be most distant from the Father's eye, was just the hour when He was in closest contact with my soul.

> —George Matheson
> (1842-1906)
> *Moments on the Mount*

Preacher and Poet

THE GRACE OF GOD IS GOD

The grace of God *is* God—God working in the soul. And He works in every soul that is willing to receive Him. That is "the Power," the strength of the believer....As we fix our thought on Him, He gains upon the soul. If we continue to seek Him, to wait upon Him, to lay open our soul to His influence, He takes a larger and larger place in our consciousness until He fills it completely....His strength, like an atmosphere wraps us round and permeates our whole spiritual life. By a thought, by fixing our heart on Him, we are lifted out of the struggle, and find refuge and peace in His presence. To be weak, to know it and to place ourselves at His disposal—that is strength.

—George Steven
(1845-1930)
Sermon: *Power from on High*

Minister, Edinburgh

YOU CANNOT FALL BENEATH THEM

Like all young men I had my temptations and sins. One day in deep remorse I went to an old cobbler, a Baptist (in Aberdeen), and asked him whether he thought it was possible for one to fall too far from God's grace. I shall never forget the look of confidence and strength which came into his strong face as he said: "Have you forgotten that *underneath are the everlasting arms? You cannot fall beneath them.* We may go down and down in sorrow or sin; but when we have gone far enough it will be to find ourselves held up by them; for we can never get beneath them; they are always beneath us."

—John Grant McKenzie
(1882-1963)
Sermon: *The Troubles of Old Age*

Professor of Psychology and Religion,
Paton College, Nottingham

THEREFORE I WAIT UPON HIM

These two things, vigilance and patience, are the main elements in the scriptural idea of waiting on God.... The name of the Lord is strength, therefore I wait on Him in the confident expectation of receiving His power. The Lord is my defence; therefore I wait on Him in the confident expectation of safety. The first name speaks of God dwelling in us, and His strength made perfect in our weakness; the second speaks of our dwelling in God, and our defencelessness sheltered in Him.

—Alexander Maclaren
(1826-1910)
Commentary: Psalm 59:9
Baptist Preacher and Expositor

I FELT HIS PRESENCE MOST

God's guiding providence of His love, leading us and fulfilling His purposes and our highest wishes by ways we knew not. I have suffered a bit, I confess, but when things were worst God was nearest. It was when I was in peril that I felt His presence most.... I never doubted, even in the darkest days, that all would come right. I had God's word for it, and that was enough for me.

—Robert Laws
(1851-1934)
*Interviewed after 45 years and
asked for deepest conviction*
Minister; Missionary, Central Africa

LET US GIVE THANKS...

I have heard that one of the Covenanters, as he walked to his death in the Grassmarket here, had only this to say, "I thank the Lord for keeping me straight." There would never have been that measure of Christian faith there is within us this night had not God by His Grace shielded us, succoured us, restrained us, guided us and brought us through all we have come through, with that little light divine still burning on the altar of our hearts....Let us give thanks for the words of Scripture that have had hands and feet to pluck at our souls; for Psalms and Hymns round which are twined sacred and dear associations; for preachers who have strengthened our feet in the way; for books that have searched and stimulated our souls; for friends who have been God's Angels in our loves; for all those ministries of God's grace whereby we have been kept in the faith.

—James Kyd Thomson
(1886-1939)
Sermon: *I Have Kept the Faith*

Minister, Mayfield

NOT TILL THEN

When I stand before the throne,
Dressed in beauty, not my own,
When I see Thee as Thou art,
Love Thee with unsinning heart,
    Then, Lord, shall I fully know,
    Not till then, how much I owe.

—Robert Murray McCheyne
(1813-1843)
Songs of Zion

Hymnologist; Minister, St. Peter's, Dundee

HE WILL NOT COME IN

And there are things we must give up and let go. God asks not for golden vessels nor vessels of silver, but he demands clean vessels. The Spirit will not come into our unclean life. He will not come into that soul that nurses a sin, secret or open, that is yet unrepented of. He will not come into a soul that has in it any root of bitterness, any envying or jealousy or malice. He will not come into any soul that still bears any grudge against a fellow-man or woman. He will not come into the soul of anyone who still indulges in any custom or habit that is even doubtful, or that may perhaps prove a stumbling-block to some weaker brother. He will not come into the soul of any who is unwilling to make a complete and absolute surrender to the will and purpose of God as it is in Jesus Christ.

> —John Robertson Sweet Wilson
> (1879-1942)
> Sermon: *The Gift of Power*

Minister, Leith

THY MIGHTY GRASP OF ME

I grasp Thy strength, make it mine own,
　　My heart with peace is blest;
I lose my hold, and then comes down
　　Darkness, and cold unrest.
Let me no more my comfort draw
　　From my frail hold of Thee,
In this alone rejoice with awe—
　　Thy mighty grasp of me.

Thy purpose of eternal good
　　Let me but surely know;
On this I'll lean—let changing mood
　　And feeling come or go—
Glad when Thy sunshine fills my soul,
　　Nor lorn when clouds o'ercast,
Since Thou within Thy sure control
　　Of love dost hold me fast.

> —John Campbell Shairp
> (1819-1885)
> *'Twixt Gleams of Joy*

Professor of Poetry, Oxford

NOTHING SO LITTLE UNDERSTOOD

Surely there is nothing so little understood as the Heart of God, else we would never be afraid to go to Him with our sins, as well as our griefs; for there is nothing in which He spends His blessed life more gladly than in pardoning and helping sinners. The largeness of His Heart does not wait till the worthiness of man can meet it. He deals with us in a way of transcendent generosity. His love is always far ahead of our prayers...and when any downcast heart cries out to Him in its sinfulness, quicker than a lightning flash His love leaps to the conclusion of mercy; and ere the broken prayer is half-uttered, the mercy is on its way.

—George H. Knight
(D. 1937)
In the Secret of His Presence
Minister, Garelochhead

BRING YOUR LEPROSY TO GOD

But let a man deal honestly with God and life, laying his soul quite open...then you will know. Your opinions about God matter little—your thoughts about religion, your arranged programme, your predetermined claim. Much of all that will have to be discarded, all of it will have to be revised, and thought will more frequently discover God by its failure than by its success. But bring your leprosy to God, and let us see Him heal it. Bring your shame and not your greatness; your bewilderment and not your fashionable opinions; your confessed folly and not your paraded cleverness. Then need will find Him where self-sufficiency must always fail. One truth of healing—a manhood cleansed and wholesome in heart—sin forgiven, morbidness gone, freshness and freedom and power returned! Behold you thought this and that and the other clever and ingenious thing. Behold now you know that your Redeemer liveth.

—John Kelman
(1864-1929)
Sermon: *Opinion and Knowledge*
Writer; Preacher, Fifth Avenue Presbyterian Church, New York

117

WHAT HAVE WE *FREELY* RECEIVED?

What have we *freely* received? Freely—(1) The knowledge of Jesus Christ *Himself* as the Son of God, the Son of Man, who has reconciled us to God, and us unto God. The Redeemer of the world. (2) We have received a free Saviour. (3) A free Spirit. The Holy Spirit free as the Saviour. (4) We have received free pardon. (5) A free Guide-Book. (6) A free way to Heaven. (7) A free entrance to glory. (8) Love, boundless, high, deep, wide, broad! Love that passes knowledge! Love that passes over our transgressions and casts our sins into the ocean. Love that renews our natures and raises us from the lowest depths to the highest Heavens. (9) Free Prayer. The Throne of Grace and Mercy open day and night, free access to the Lord God Almighty through the blood of the Lamb. . . . The way is open, free!

> —Lady Grisell Baillie
> (1822-1891)
> Sermon: *Freely Ye Have Received*

Devotional Writer; First Deaconess of the Church of Scotland

GOD EXCLUDES NONE...

I say, God is the hope of His people, and not their own holiness. . . . Now, when men place their hope in any other thing besides the Lord, it is no wonder they are kept in a staggering condition. . . . They complain that they know not whether they be in Christ or not; but as few take pains to be in Him, so few take pains to try if they be in Him. It is a work and business which cannot be done sleeping. . . . God excludes none, if they do not exclude themselves. *If any man will,* he shall be welcome. We say, then, it is a most necessary duty thus to close with Christ Jesus, as the blessed relief appointed for sinners.

> —William Guthrie
> (1620-1665)
> *The Christian's Great Interest*

Minister of Fenwick

PATIENT ENDURANCE

The grace of God will do very little for us if we resolve to do nothing for ourselves. God calls us to co-operate with Him in the perfecting of character. And we must discipline ourselves. We must get down to the business of life. We must come to see where we are weak where we should be strong, and where we are strong where we should be weak. We must school ourselves. We must penalise ourselves. Nobody else can do it, and God will not. It is your business, and it is mine. There must with this also be patient endurance. Endurance is a most striking quality. Without it the most commendable efforts of men must prove futile. "He that shall endure unto the end, the same shall be saved."

—William Graham Scroggie
(1877-1958)
Baptist Minister, Charlotte Chapel, Edinburgh; Principal, Spurgeon's College

A WEARISOME SERVITUDE

Objects of enjoyment may be presented to us; but without a capacity suited to them, they can yield us no pleasure. Musical sounds charm not him who is deaf and beauty has no attraction to the blind. In like manner, true happiness cannot be relished by the wicked. The joys of heaven a proud, a sensual, or a worldly spirit is not capable of tasting. To dwell with a God whom we do not love, and to whom we cannot in everything submit...would prove a wearisome servitude, and an unceasing source of misery.

—Robert Coutts
(1771-1803)
Sermon: *Matthew 16:24*
Minister at Brechin

PROVIDENCE STRIKES US MORE READILY

We...can recall things in our history which we cannot but regard as providential, determining our course in life and leading us on towards the place which we are going to occupy....The things we remember may be small, indeed trifles; but when we take a broad view of life, they acquire a greater magnitude. Our minds were perhaps fixed on a certain career in life, but in order to pursue it, it was necessary that we should gain some distinction in learning, or obtain some position, and we failed; and the failure altered our whole career; and now we are where we are, about to enter a calling more sacred. Providence of the kind, being internal, strike us more readily; and reflecting on them does enable us to find God in our life. Indeed, though we ordinarily overlook such things from want of thought, when we are led more seriously to consider our history, we find it full of them.

> —Andrew Bruce Davidson
> (1831-1902)
> *Lecture on Jeremiah*

Professor of Theology, Glasgow

WE MIGHT READ AND FIND OUT

If this fair volume which we "World" do name,
    If we the sheets and leaves could turn with care!
Of Him Who it corrects, and did it frame,
    We clear might read the art and wisdom rare,
Find out His power, which widest powers doth tame,
    His providence extending everywhere.

> —William Drummond of Hawthornden
> (1585-1649)
> *The World*

Poet and Preacher

NOT THE PRIZE OF A LOFTY INTELLECT

But the gospel is no such system of high and abstract truth. The salvation it offers is not the prize of a lofty intellect, but of a lowly heart. The mirror in which its grand truths are reflected is not a mind of calm and philosophic abstraction, but a heart of earnest purity. Its light shines best and fullest, not on a life undisturbed by business, but on a soul unstained by sin. The religion of Christ, while it affords scope for the loftiest intellect in the contemplation and development of its glorious truths, is yet, in the exquisite simplicity of its essential facts and principles patent to the simplest mind. Rude, untutored, toil-worn you may be, but if you have wit enough to guide you in the commonest round of daily toil, you have wit enough to learn to be saved. The truth as it is in Jesus, while, in the view of it, so profound that the highest archangel's intellect may be lost in the contemplation of its mysterious depths, is yet, in another, so simple that the lisping babe at a mother's knee may learn its meaning.

—John Caird
(1820-1898)
Sermon: *Religion in Common Life*
Principal, Glasgow University

GOD MADE INTELLIGIBLE

So long as we refuse to look at Christ we may truly say we see little to persuade us to be religious, little evidence of a God we can worship. But in Christ we do find a God before whom reason, conscience, heart alike bow and claim as our Supreme. In Christ we have the God who is past finding out made intelligible, manifest in the flesh. In Christ we find what proclaims itself divine, a God in whom we see that infinite greatness is infinite capacity of love and service, a God who applies His resources without stint to the actual needs of His creatures, and finds in their guilty entanglements and hopeless misery but a fit field for the ampler operation of His love; who teaches us by actual demonstration that it is more blessed to give than to receive. In Christ we see that which makes religion possible, inevitable, reasonable, and full of blessedness.

—Marcus Dods
(1834-1909)
Sermon: *Why Be Religious?*
Professor of New Testament Exegesis, Edinburgh

FEW STAND AND GAZE

Times of worship are occasions when a man is brought face to face with the facts of his own life. In business he has no time to remember them, in pleasure his anxiety is to forget. Few men, apart from the hours of worship, ever stand and gaze before the facts of birth and death, before their own pitifulness and splendour, their transience and their permanence. Yet all men know that it is only those who take thought upon these things who grow in wisdom.

—John Robert Paterson Sclater
(1878-1949)
Sermon
Minister, North United Free Church, Edinburgh

WE WORSHIP GOD BECAUSE

Insolent in prosperity and craven in adversity, such men betray that they have no reverence, nothing which prescribes justice and mercy as the only enduring foundations of power, nothing therefore which can be a support to them in their own time of weakness. Against all this world exiled Israel sets its humble and unhesitating answer: we worship God because of what we believe about Him, not because of what we believe about you. Finding in Him a control, we also find in Him a support.

—Adam C. Welch
(1864-1943)
Visions of the End
Professor of Hebrew, Edinburgh

WE WAIT FOR GOD

We wait for God; not for men, not for crowds, not for eloquence, not for emotion or sensation, but for God. Our hope is in the Living God, and we wait with hushed spirits to hear what He will say, and in obedience to do it.

—Donald Fraser
(1870-1933)
*Prayer at Student Volunteer
Movement*
Minister; Missionary, Livingstonia, Central Africa

WORSHIP IS THE
TRANSCENDENT WONDER...

Worship is the transcendent wonder of men and women who
know that life is more than maps and measurements, data and
statistics, timetables and graphs. Christian worship is our
wonder and amazement at the gift of God in Jesus Christ our
Lord, our openness to the presence and power of the Holy
Spirit and our glimpse of the world unseen through simple
elements as water, bread, and wine. These things are too
wonderful for me. I do not understand. But through them you
and I may find the gift that alone can satisfy the soul—"the
peace of God that passeth *all* understanding."

> —David Haxton Carswell Read
> (1910-   )
> Sermon: *On Explaining Everything*

Minister, Madison Avenue Presbyterian Church, New York

SENSE OF SWEET FELLOWSHIP

I spent the Sundays of that year, doggedly fighting my way back
to life again. I had my books and revelled in them. I had my ear
to the very heart of Nature. But I shall never forget, as long as I
live, the deep delicious filling of the heart that came to me on the
first Lord's Day when I joined again in worship with God's
people. It was not the sermon that made the waters rise. I have
certainly forgotten what it was about. It was certainly not the
excitement of the crowd, for the Highland sanctuary was far
from crowded. It was the sense of sweet fellowship, of sweet
communion, of spiritual reinforcement and support in the
gathering together of God's people.

> —George H. Morrison
> (1866-1928)
> *Moderatorial Address to the*
> *General Assembly*

Minister, Wellington, Glasgow

IF GOD DID NOT CARE

If God did not care for our souls He would not care for ourselves. He would be setting at naught the very nature He has made. Not to care for our words would be not to care for the elevation and fervour of our souls, not to care for our words would be not to care for our strivings and aspirations, for our burdens and fears and sorrows.... Nay, the Father seeketh to be worshipped. He is love. He is no cold motionless abstraction, but a living heart. He seeks to be worshipped because He seeks the heart. Therefore...pour out your hearts before Him.

—Joseph Leckie
(1826-1889)
Sermon: *Worship*

Minister, Ibrox, Glasgow

ONLY THOU, O GOD, ALONE

'Twas neither righteous men nor great
But God a refuge found for me.
No man in this world can me teach,
But only Thou, O God, alone.
None keepeth truth but Heaven's King;
To His wisdom none is like.
If I am in the way of truth,
My tonsure-vow requites it all.
If, O Trinity, on a lie I rest,
Lead me into the way of truth.

—Assigned to
Muireach Albannach
(1180-*c*. 1220)
(Earliest Gaelic Poet)

Translated by Thomas M'lauchlan

ALL FACTS ARE FACTS OF GOD

The nearer we are to Christ, the more we live under His influence, the more open-minded we can afford to be to all new facts, if they are facts, to all new truth, if it is true. He shows us that all facts are facts of God, that all truths are truths of God, from whatever source they may be revealed. Above all, He convinces us that still and for ever, He holds the key to all the secrets that matter most.

—George Sinclair Gunn
(1900-1961)
Sermon: *The Indispensable Christ*
Minister, Broughton Place, Edinburgh

COME AS POOR AND NEEDY

To all, then, who want a religion, to all who are seekers after God, to all who believe in God, but know not how to find him, I would say, "Come unto Jesus; He is 'the Way, the Truth, and the Life.' Come, all ye who labour and are heavy laden, and He will give you rest. Come in sincerity, come in earnestness, come renouncing all self-righteousness, and all other ways of coming unto God; come, as poor, and needy, and helpless, and you shall not come in vain. He will receive you graciously and love you freely. He will enlighten your understandings, calm your consciences, purify your affections, and gladden your hearts."

—William Lindsay Alexander
(1808-1884)
Sermon: *The Sacrifice of Christ*
Minister, Edinburgh

SINNERS, THINK OF THIS

Know then, O sinners! that, after all the contempt you have thrown upon Him He is still willing to become your Saviour. Ungrateful as you have been, He once more opens His arms, and invites you to come unto Him....Behold, in the Gospel offer, He lays, as it were, His crucified body in your way, to stop you in your self-destroying course And will you still press onward, "and trample under-foot the Son of God?"...O, sinners, think of this! all who perish under the Gospel must carry this dreadful aggravation along with them: that mercy was in their offer, and they would not accept it; nay, that they insulted and abused the mercy that would have saved them.

—Robert Walker
(1716-1783)
Sermon: *The Heavy Laden Invited to Christ*
Minister, High Kirk, Edinburgh

BE WILLING TO BE CLEANSED

Ability to obey begins with the new birth, but, if ever we are to be saved from the tyranny of sin, we must be willing to be enabled. Once, in the days of the Scottish Covenant, John Blackadder, of saintly memory, was preaching in the fields. He held up Christ to the people, charging them to receive and embrace Him. One of His hearers, standing far in the rear, called to the preacher across the crowd, 'Hold your hand, sir: I give my consent.' This is what God requires. Your feelings may be languid, your repentance may be feeble, your faith may be dim, but, give *your consent*. Tell God that you are willing—sincerely and heartily willing to be saved.

—David M. McIntyre
(1859-1938)
The Way of Salvation
Principal, Bible Training Institute, Glasgow

BREATHE WITH HIS HEART

And what have you got to do? Just to take Him into your inmost heart, to choose henceforth not to do what you like yourself, but what Jesus would have done. To feel to your fellow-men as He felt. To believe about God and in a simple, loving way, to go through this world following in His sweet footsteps, and really trying to understand what He was, and to get His Spirit and heart into you, and to make your life breathe with His heart and His holiness.

—William Gray Elmslie
(1848-1889)
Sermon: *Not Your Own*
Professor of Hebrew, Presbyterian College, London

THEY SIMPLY FOLLOWED

The first disciples did not receive their new life-changing thoughts of God and Man, of the Incarnation, the Atonement, the Eternal Kingdom, at second-hand. They simply followed Christ, and out of the life of following their creed grew inevitably, and with it their power to put it forth in action. Nothing gives this power save this companionship, this friendship of heart with heart: no mere record, no creed at second-hand, nothing but Himself. "Come unto me"; "abide in me"; "without me ye can do nothing"; "if a man love me, he will keep my words": all these sayings prove that Christ saw His own personality alone had power to transform the soul.

—John Smyth Carroll
(1853-1923)
Sermon: *Follow Me*
Minister, St. John's, Glasgow

REMEMBER OUR EXAMPLE

It was only, let us remember, because Christ retired frequently into a solitary place and prayed that He, the Lord of us all, was enabled to fulfil the mission of our redemption. He withdrew Himself into these lonely colloquies with the Father not because He was weary of His work, but that He might be the better equipped for it. And he returned to it with a clearer purpose and baptised with new power. He has left us an example, that we should follow in His steps; and thus gain, from the sterner visions of solitude, guidance and strength to make our life a Divine service and a pilgrimage to the City of Light.

—David William Forrest
(1856-1918)
Sermon: *The Vision of Loneliness*

Professor of Theology, Glasgow

CHRIST'S RELIANCE

Again, the example of Christ emphasizes that success comes through the use of means. No one was more diligent than He, in increasing faith or in yielding Himself to the leading of God, and the discipline of daily duty. But Christ relied upon two things—the Word of God and prayer. Difficult as it may be for us to grasp all that prayer and the Scriptures were to Christ, yet the impression which we carry away from the Gospels is, that these were the means through which He drew His power and fed His life. If we want our life to be strong and our service to be fruitful, we too must use the means that will promote them.

—Adam Philip
(1856-1945)
Sermon: *The Father's Hand*

Minister, Longforgan

THE LORD LAID OPEN TO ME

In Ireland the Lord laid open to me the understanding of my
unbelief, so that I might at last face up to my wickedness and be
converted with all my heart to the Lord my God. He respected
my humiliation and had mercy on my youth and ignorance.
Even before I knew Him, He watched over me. Before I was
able to tell good from evil, He protected me and comforted me
as a father would his son.

—St. Patrick
(*c.* 389-*c.* 461)
His Confession

Translated from the Latin

MY WEB OF TIME HE WOVE

O Christ! He is the fountain
　　The deep sweet well of love;
The streams on earth I've tasted
　　More deep I'll drink above:
There to an ocean fulness
　　His mercy doth expand,
And glory, glory dwelleth
　　In Immanuel's land.

With mercy and with judgment
　　My web of time He wove,
And aye the dews of sorrow
　　Were lustred by His love;
I'll bless the hand that guided,
　　I'll bless the heart that planned,
When throned where glory dwelleth
　　In Immanuel's land.

—Anne Ross Cousin
(1824-1906)
Immanuel's Land and Other Poems

Devotional Poet

EFFICIENCY AND SUFFICIENCY

There is all efficiency and sufficiency in Jesus Christ to crown the work of grace and complete what He has begun. Whether, therefore, you want more faith, purity of heart or peace of mind, more light or love, a humbler or a holier spirit, a calmer or a tenderer conscience, a livelier sense of Christ's excellencies or of your own unworthiness, fear not to ask too much. With a well ever full and ever flowing, our vessels need never be empty. No earthly fortune will stand daily visits to the bank, but this will. You may go too seldom, you cannot go too often, to the throne; you may ask too little, you cannot ask too much; for in Jesus dwelleth all the fulness of the Godhead bodily.

—Thomas Guthrie
(1803-1873)
Sermon: *The Fulness That Is in Christ*

Preacher and Philanthropist

HUMAN NEEDS WILL NOT ALTER

Subtlest thought shall fail, and learning falter,
Churches change, forms perish, systems go;
But our human needs they will not alter;
Christ no human age shall e'er outgrow.

Yea, Amen! O changeless One, Thou only
Art life's Guide and spiritual goal,
Thou, the light across the dark vale lonely,
Thou, the eternal haven of the soul.

—John Campbell Shairp
(1819-1885)

Professor of Poetry, Oxford

HE WOULD HAVE DONE FAR MORE

What is this but to say that the sources of our very life are in Christ's keeping, not in ours? He guards for us the springs of faith and love. The reservoir in which our supplies are stored is yonder, not here; and enough for each day's necessity is given. All that Christ has, He has for those who love Him; and one sometimes imagines that His greatest sorrow, if perchance He sorrows still, must be that we draw upon Him so sparingly, with the fear lest we are asking too much.... Never judge of your Redeemer's grace and power by what you have yet received from Him. Had you suffered Him, He would have done far more.

—Hugh Ross Mackintosh
(1870-1936)
Sermon: *The Hidden Life*
Professor of Systematic Theology, Edinburgh

GRACE AND TRUTH BECAME ONE

Nor can I conclude without a reference to Him in whom grace and truth became one, whose life was truth in love, who is the way, the truth, and the life, in whom are hid all the treasures of wisdom and of knowledge, who is the realised ideal of humanity. Nay, He is more: He is set for the making of men, for the help and strengthening of men into the higher life; who can and does pour into our broken lives the fulness of His own gracious life, who can make us men indeed.

—James Iverach
(1839-1922)
Sermon: *To University of
Edinburgh, 1911*
Professor, New Testament, Aberdeen

HIGHEST AMOUNT OF PERSONAL HOLINESS

I am persuaded that I shall obtain the highest amount of personal holiness, I shall do most for God's glory and the good of men, and I shall have the fullest reward in eternity by maintaining a conscience always washed in the blood of Christ, by being filled with the Holy Spirit at all times, and attaining the most entire likeness to Christ in my will and heart that it is possible for a redeemed sinner to attain in this world.

—Robert Murray McCheyne
(1813-1843)
Letters

Hymnologist; Minister, St. Peter's, Dundee

THE GLORY EXTOLLED

Where is all the glory that is so much extolled? For discovering this, faith needs only look through this thin veil of flesh; and under that low disguise appears the Lord of glory, the King of kings, the Lord of hosts strong and mighty, the Lord mighty in battle; the heavens His throne, the earth His footstool, the light His garments, the clouds His chariots, the thunder His voice, His strength omnipotence, His riches all-sufficiency, His glory infinite, His retinue the hosts of heaven, and the excellent ones of the earth, on whom He bestows riches unsearchable, an inheritance incorruptible, banquets of everlasting joys, and preferments of immortal honour, making them kings and priests unto God, conquerors, yea, and more than conquerors, children of God, and mystically one *with* Himself.

—John Maclaurin
(1693-1754)
Sermon: *Glorying in the Cross of Christ*

Minister, Glasgow

THE LIFE IS IN THE BLOOD

Medical Science is unable to locate in any one organ the actual seat of human life. The most accurate description a Physiologist could give would be to state that life is "wherever the blood is." In other words, "The life is in the blood," just as scripture has stated. Blood is a living fluid, with "life-giving" properties. In these days of blood transfusion we do not need to have this argued to us. The blood serum is a medium, bearing the principle and all the necessities for life. There is a sense in which we may reverently say that our union with Christ has brought us a life-saving transfusion from the life which is beyond the grave. The shedding of Christ's blood, the pouring out of His life, has bestowed upon the men who have come to Him the energising principle of the life to come.

—Duncan M. Blair
(1896-1944)
Via, Veritas, Vita
Professor of Anatomy, University of Glasgow

LOST CHILDREN RANSOMED

When God brings back His ransomed children He changes their natures, so that from being alienated from Him they are made to love Him. When he puts forth the power of His grace upon them He makes them willing to serve Him. "A new heart will I give you," He says, "and a new spirit will I put within you; and I will cause you to walk in My statutes, and ye shall keep My commandments and do them." Thus the lost children, ransomed by the blood of Jesus, are restored to freedom, to obedience, and to happiness everlasting.

—George Simmie Smith
(1822-1899)
Sermon: *The Victory Over Sin and Death*
Minister, Cranstoun

THE PAST AS STARTING-POINT

We cannot undo the past and begin afresh. We have to take the past as the starting-point and determining element of the future. We are what the past has made us; and the memory of former things is indelible. But the Gospel reminds us that what cannot be obliterated may be transmuted by grace. In Christ we may become new creatures; and in the eternal life that we begin, in union with Him, all old things, so far as there is any condemning power in them, pass away, and all things in the transfiguring light of heavenly love become new.

—Hugh Macmillan
(1833-1903)
Sermon: *The Permanence of the Past*

Minister, Greenock

WE ARE COMPLETE IN HIM

We are complete in Him as regards the certainty of our final sanctification and blessedness. The end of our faith is the salvation of the soul in its complete deliverance from the taint and blight of sin. As the seed contains in embryo the full-grown and perfect tree, the germ of faith contains the perfect beauty of holiness. From the first step to the last the progress of the believer onwards to the consummation of his spiritual being is guarded and settled by every security that God's promise can give, and His power to redeem. If we are complete in Him, surely He deserves a complete trust, a complete love, a complete obedience, a firm cleaving to Him, a continual abiding in Him so as to draw forth into our hearts that vital influence through which the spirit lives and grows.

—James Drummond Burns
(1823-1864)
Sermon: *Complete In Him*

Minister, Hampstead, London

IN HIM LOVE STOOD...

His suffering therefore was not passion merely: it was action in the highest degree. Our Redeemer stood alone in the universe as the visible exponent of love. Earth rejected Him, Hell assailed Him, Heaven forsook Him. He took to Himself the arm of strength, and broke the tyranny of the evil one. He made an end of sin and finished the transgression. The pitiless reed was His sceptre of dominion, the robe of mockery was His mantle of power, the wreath of thorns was the diadem of all-embracing empire, the rough-hewn cross was His triumphal chariot on which He rode to glory. In Him love stood with its back to the wall fighting for dear life—and it won through.

> —David M. McIntyre
> (1859-1938)
> *Faith's Title Deeds*
> Principal, Bible Training Institute, Glasgow

ON THE THRESHOLD

This young man is a type of very many, a type of the better class of minds. A man of high and lovely character, yet feeling that his character was not enough, whose very elevation of character put out its hands, and groped for something better than itself—a man dissatisfied, dissatisfied with the world, and yet unable to give it up; dissatisfied, with himself, and yearning for something higher; feeling something in him that was empty and that yearned and craved to be filled—such a man on the threshold of the kingdom of God, earnestly entreated by Christ to enter, entreated with a look that said He loved him—and yet turning away!

> —Andrew Bruce Davidson
> (1831-1902)
> Sermon: *The Rich Young Ruler*
> Professor of Theology, Glasgow

CHRIST WITHIN AND ABOUT

Christ as a Light, illumine and guide me,
Christ as a shield o'ershadow and cover me,
Christ be under me, Christ be over me,
Christ be beside me on left hand and right,
Christ be before, behind me, about me,
Christ this day be within and without me.

—St. Patrick
(*c.* 389-*c.* 461)

Prayer before going to Ireland

DOING DESPITE TO THE SPIRIT

The River is not a private aqueduct; it flows not through some conserved limits, within which the privileged few are permitted to appear. It is a river which has flowed from the beginning, which has not been fenced off nor enclosed,—neither, indeed, can or shall be,—and which shall continue to roll its ever-increasing volume, onwards and onwards, through every land,—open and free to all who will partake of it. This we proclaim! The Spirit and the Bride have said "Come"; and the sin of all invited hearers of the Gospel is, that they have hitherto refused to come; that they have rejected Christ and His fulness; that they have done or are doing despite to the Spirit of Grace. *Return; come!*

—Alexander Beith
(1799-1891)
Sermon: *The River of Water of Life*

Minister, Stirling

THE GREAT DIVIDE AMONG MEN

In heaven's eyes the Great Divide among men is not between rich and poor, learned and unlearned, or any other standard of classification which counts for so much in the eyes of this world, but between those who accept and those who reject His Word in Christ. Blessed are we if, standing before the Cross of Jesus, we have found that there our Father has come out to meet us through the storm and to bring us safely home.

> —Daniel Lamont
> (1869-1950)
> Sermon: *The Love Incomparable*
> Professor of Practical Theology, Edinburgh

KNOW HIM...

Know God in Christ as the God of your conscience, Whose mercy in the cross has silenced the voice of guilt and awakened in you the love of holiness. Know Him as the indwelling Spirit Who inspires and answers your prayers. Know Him with the spirit as a daily Familiar—the best of Fathers and the most steadfast of Friends. Get into links of confidential fellowship with the Eternal, so that you cannot for a moment question His nearness without denying your own deepest experience. Then no intellectual difficulty can rob you of Him. The sanctuary of the intellect may be pillaged; but the sanctuary of the devout spirit, of the new life born of God, never! "He that believeth hath the witness in himself."

> —James Oswald Dykes
> (1835-1912)
> Sermon: *Robbed of One's Gods*
> Professor; Principal, English Presbyterian College

NONE BUT CHRIST!

The doctrine of Christ will not avail instead. I can never rest upon a creed, however true. Even the word of Christ in this Holy Bible will not avail instead. How can I build for eternity upon a word-foundation merely? I need the Redeemer Himself, more than even His doctrine of redemption—the Saviour Himself, more than even His promise of salvation. I am most thankful for the balm of Gilead, but I do not know how I am myself to use it. Oh, for the good Physician to come in person with it for my care. The All in all of faith, the All in all of assurance too, is none other than Himself. I will have no faith and no assurance, which may allow me to think that I can be safe in any other way than that of immediate and absolute dependence upon Christ, upon Christ alone.

—Edward A. Thomson
(1817-1890)
Sermon: *The Assurance of Faith*
Minister, Free St. Stephen's Church, Edinburgh

MY OFT REFRAIN

Each day I count Thy sweets and mercies
And me to heed Thy holy laws
A song for every love-gift chanting,
Be I Thy harper without pause.

Each dawn more love to Thee, O Jesus,
I offer, and each eve again;
Each day and night, each dark and light
Be this desire my oft refrain.

—Chanted Gaelic Prayer
(16th century)
Translated by Alistair Maclean

SELF-LOVE OR REAL LOVE?

There may be a kind of sentimental love, spending much time in the closet, reading books of devotion, waiting much on public means of grace, writing letters or making entries in journals that seem to breathe the spirit of love. In all which there may be more self-love with self-pleasing than real love to Christ....No depth of mere emotion, no temporary outburst of feeling, will take the place of an honest, hearty, painstaking endeavour to please and obey and serve. It is a poor love that can make no surrender of the will, no sacrifice of personal ease and comfort, no earnest effort to help others or bring glory to Christ in the advancement of His cause.

> —James Hood Wilson
> (1829-1903)
> *His last sermon: John 14*

Minister, Barclay, Edinburgh

PARDONED ... TO PROCLAIM

I am persuaded that there is not anything that a pardoned sinner does not desire more, than to magnify and speak much of that Free Grace; he is not backward to send others to that door where he found grace, and, I think, if such a one could gather all the earth together, and have a stance to be seen of all, and a voice to be heard of all, this would be the thing that he would proclaim to them, the riches of Free Grace, and would invite them all to come in.

> —Robert Leighton
> (1611-1684)
> *Sermon* (1643)

Archbishop of Glasgow; Professor; Minister at Dunblane

IT IS BY CONFESSION

The fear of being charged with egotism must not be allowed to silence your testimony to the saving mercy of Christ which you have experienced. Nor must you wait for the fulness and maturity of the Christian life before you publicly acknowledge Him. It is by confession, not by concealment, that you gain strength. Cowardice is cured out in the open. Faith unacknowledged is like a plant which grows in the dark. It is pale and sickly. Barren of bright blossoms or healthy fruit, it ultimately droops and dies. You are not told in Scripture that you are to bear testimony when you have overcome, but to overcome by the word of your testimony.

—Alexander Frazer of Tain
(1870-1964)
Sermon: *Never Despair!*

Preacher and Evangelist

A SAVIOUR FAR AWAY

There are many reasons why men do not love the Lord Jesus. Some feel no need of Him. They understand that He is a Saviour; but a Saviour is what they do not desire. Others have no congeniality with Him. They understand that His character is divine—that His love of holiness is so intense as His hatred of iniquity—and as they love the world, and love their own way and love the pleasures of sin, they can not love the Lord Jesus. But the hearts of some toward Christ are cold for other reasons. Their conceptions regarding Him are sufficiently vague and dim; but so far as they can be reduced to any thing definite, we might say that they do not love the Lord Jesus, because they habitually think of Him as a dead Saviour, or a Saviour different from what He was, or a distant Saviour—a Saviour far away.

—James Hamilton
(1810-1867)
Sermon: *The Parting Promise*

Minister, Strathaven

RELIGION IN THE SOUL

Carry holy principles with you into the world and the world will become hallowed by your presence. A Christ-like spirit will Christianize every thing it touches. A meek heart, in which the altar-fire of love to God is burning, will lay hold of the commonest, rudest things in life, and transmute them, like coarse fuel at the touch of fire, into a pure and holy flame.... Religion in the soul will make all the work and toil of life—its gains and losses, friendships, rivalries, competitions, its manifold incidents and events—the means of religious advancement.... To spiritualize what is material, to Christianize what is secular—this is the noble achievement of Christian principle.

> —John Caird
> (1820-1898)
> Sermon: *Religion in Common Life*
Principal, Glasgow University

CHRISTIANITY DOES NOT MEAN

Christianity does not mean the recognition of necessary truths of reason, but an attitude of the soul to God, determined by Christ; and history is not to the religious man a chapter of accidents, but the stage on which a Divine purpose is achieved which could not be more ineptly described than by calling it accidental. Religion can no more be simplified by making it independent of history than respiration would be simplified by soaring above the atmosphere.

> —James Denney
> (1856-1917)
> *Jesus and the Gospel*
Professor of Theology, Glasgow

CHRISTIANITY IS A NECESSITY

Christianity is a necessity because the grimmer side of life makes it so for us. Trouble and tragedy have a manifold effect on our religious life. On the one hand, they make it more difficult for us to believe in God; on the other, they make it indispensable that we should believe in Him.... In the dark days that come to us all, how can we keep our sanity, how can we remain unembittered, how can we be a strength and not a weakness to others—unless we can draw near to Jesus Christ and receive from Him the strength and peace He has been giving perplexed and troubled souls for more than nineteen hundred years? When we think of the tasks and burdens facing us, is there any one of us who does not find himself constrained to say, 'I need Jesus Christ'?

> —Ian Henderson
> (1910-1960)
> Sermon: *Four Theories About Christianity*

Preacher and Professor of Religion, Glasgow

PAUL HAD IT

Preaching is a good work, yet there are many preachers that had not a good testimony from their conscience, in that good work; but Paul had it; and that which made him to have it, was his sincerity and singleness; that he spoke as before God, in the sight of God.... If we could preach and pray, and live and walk thus in all our actions, O! what sweet peace should we have, living and dying.

> —James Durham
> (1622-1658)
> Sermon: *Romans 9:9*

Minister, Glasgow

WERE THEY STUBBORN, OR...

I am of the opinion, brother, that you were more severe to your unlearned hearers than you ought to have been, and did not at first, comformably to the apostolic rule, give them the milk of more easy doctrine, till being by degrees nourished with the Word of God, they should be capable to greater perfection and be able to practise God's sublimest precepts.... Brother, were they stubborn, or you hard?

—St. Aidan
(*c.* 580-651)
On hearing Colman's Report
(Colman sent on mission to Northumbria, 635 A.D.; returned, reported to Iona Monks of his failure)

THEY SUBSTITUTE COLD KNOWLEDGE

They substitute cold knowledge for the light which cometh from above; and venture to teach others by proclaiming to them tidings which they themselves have never known. True, there may be much knowledge and learning in their heads and a fluent tongue as well. They may be loud-voiced, and their sermons may be most exactly in their memories, and as polished as if they had smoothed them with a plane. But how can they proclaim the gospel in all its glory and its power, with a dark understanding, a hard heart, and an insensate conscience. For though the blind may speak of colours, he never saw their beauty; and though a bird may utter words, it knows nothing of their meaning.

—John McDonald
(1779-1849)
Tribute to Missionary at Achreny
Minister; "Apostle of the North"

WE PREACH NOT OURSELVES

We preach not ourselves, therefore, but Christ Jesus the Lord, this promised Messiah, this blessed Saviour, this glorious Sovereign of our souls. We preach not our own opinions, but His gospel. We preach it as delivered in the sacred scriptures, not as it is sophisticated by the comments, or perverted by the depravity of men. We preach all its compass, and extent, not such parts of it only as appear agreeable to our own preconceived tenets, or favourable to the sect which we have embraced. We preach it, not with a view to sanction, by divine authority, our own dogmatical system, whatever it may be, but to submit, to the test of divine truth, every sentiment we entertain, every doctrine we deliver, every precept we inculcate. What the sacred oracles sanction not, we disclaim. What they dictate we believe, maintain, and enforce.

—William Laurence Brown
(1755-1830)
Sermon: *August 23, 1795*
Principal, Marischal College, Aberdeen

IF YOU WISH TO MOVE US

You ministers should have more of the infinite in your sermons.... If you wish to move us, you must make us feel that you see more than you are able to express, and that you think and know that there is an infinite height and depth beyond what you see. But you go to the brim of the great ocean, you dip your tumbler into it, and set it down before us, and you tell us "that's the ocean."

—Alexander Moody Stuart
(1809-1898)
*Moderatorial Address to
General Assembly, 1875*
Minister, St. Luke's, Edinburgh (Quoting an Elder)

BEFORE HIM THAT SENT ME

My sermons must be read before Him that sent me to preach, for Hee will know how I have fedde His Lambes.... God giveth to no man heere all good things at once; but some we receive in hand and some in hope....Heaven is not winne with a wish....Throw many tribulation the Crowne is after a course of crosses....A sinne well confessed is healed....Death cometh upon man with stealing steps.

—Zachary Boyd
(1585?-1653)
The Last Battell of the Soul
(Published 1629)
Minister, Namur, France, and Barony, Glasgow

FLOWERING OR FROTHING OF MIND

Authentic personal experience gives to any utterance on any subject a power of assault and a skill of entry derivable from no other source; and this applies in a special way to the realm of religion, the subject-matter of which is precisely the truth of personal existence. Very quickly, as you listen to a preacher, you begin to sense whether his words are the flowering of a life or just the frothing of a mind; whether he is a genuine traveller or only a clerk in the office of Thomas Cook & Son.* You feel this whether or not he is a good preacher in a superficial sense.

—Archibald Campbell Craig
(1888-   )
Preaching in a Scientific Age

Preacher, Lecturer, Writer
*Travel agents in Britain

MEN STILL FLOCK

All preachers cannot have the genius of their masters, but they can have their diligence, their brooding solitude, their ascent of the heights. The simple message is still listened to if it is brought as a living Word. Men still flock where an authentic voice is heard. And they still want to hear of the great themes: the wonder of forgiveness; the glories of creation—in an age that has uncovered so much; the austerity of Jesus; the Immortal Hope; the meaning of the Cross; the work of the Spirit; retribution with its tale of inevitable sowing and reaping.

—Robert Henry Wishart Shepherd
(1888-1970)
Under the Oaks
Principal, Lovedale College, South Africa

September 30

THAT MAN SHOWED ME

I came to Irvine, and heard a well-favoured, proper old man (David Dickson), with a long beard, and that man showed me all my heart. Then I went to St. Andrews, where I heard a sweet, majestic-looking man (Robert Blair), and he showed me the majesty of God. After him, I heard a little fair man (Samuel Rutherford), and he showed me the loveliness of Christ.

—Robert Wodrow
(1679-1734)
Analecta
Minister; Historian, Glasgow

WE SOW POTATOES WE REAP POTATOES

It is well to remember that our own reactions to life will determine the kind of vessel God can make. God cannot be mocked: it is still true that we reap what we sow; and that it is not a sign of an angry or an unjust God. Rather it is the proof that we live in an ordered universe. I see too many people who rail against the fruits which their own fault has compelled them to reap. But surely our hope of the world is that if we sow potatoes we reap potatoes and not turnips. We cannot barter our conscience and have peace; we cannot barter purity and then expect to be as though we had never sinned. Nor must we expect that when we do turn to God there will be no struggle to keep close to Him. We must be satisfied to be *another vessel,* not what God could and would have made us if we had not sinned.

—John Grant McKenzie
(1882-1963)
Personal Problems of Conduct and Religion
Professor of Psychology and Religion, Patton College, Nottingham

GOD GIVES US STONES

It is one primal tenet of my belief that God gives us all, the stones to build our lives and we can do with them one of two things. We can build a high containing wall round our own happiness, to the shutting out of God and man, only to witness a garden becoming a desert and the soul within dying the death. Or on the other we can take the stones He puts into our hands and from them build a bridge into other less privileged lives, so that daily we pass over it on errands of love and mercy.

—George Johnstone Jeffrey
(1881-1961)
It's My Belief (B.B.C.)
Minister, Glasgow; Warrack Lecturer

OUR LIFE'S CHIEF BUSINESS

As a Christian reviews his life from time to time, what comes home to him with overwhelming power is that his best committal was but a poor thing, and that God was repeatedly shaming his half-heartedness by the generosity of His dealing. The rescue from a temptation with which he had trifled too long, the gift of an unselfish friend, the wonder of a human love that looks fearlessly at all faults and still cares—these and much else are rightly interpreted as part of God's gracious action towards His child. It is *this* that stirs us to penitence and to what grows out of genuine penitence, the surrender which is both the yearning and the resolve to be so knit with God that the doing of His will becomes the chief business of our lives.

—Charles Sim Duthie
(1911-   )
God in His World
Principal of New College, University of London

ISSUES OF EARTHLY LIFE

Are we not led often to treat this earthly life as an education, not as a probation at all—to lose the sense of the awful issues with which it is weighted? We may not be in a position to speak very definitely as to all that is implied in the transition from this world to another, but we do justice neither to the New Testament nor to the witness of conscience unless in our preaching we put the emphasis of moral decision within the present life.

—David William Forrest
(1856-1918)
Evangelicalism
Professor of Theology, Glasgow

EVERY MAN IS A MISSIONARY

Every man is a missionary, now and forever, for good or for evil, whether he intends or designs it or not. He may be a blot radiating his dark influence outward to the very circumference of society, or he may be a blessing spreading benediction over the length and breadth of the world. But a blank he cannot be, there are no moral blanks, there are no neutral characters. We are either the sower that sows and corrupts, or the light that steadily illuminates.

—Thomas Chalmers
(1780-1847)
Mathematician, Preacher, Leader

WHAT THEN?

The world is entitled to look to us for light: but what if the world looking, should find nothing distinctive in our practical life; nothing in our estimate and use of money, nothing in our choice of friends, no preference of the nobler and higher ends of life, little pronounced sympathy with goodness, little compassion for sorrow and sin, little simplicity and elevation of character, little of strength, endeavour and victory: what then?

—Robert Rainy
(1826-1906)
Sermon: *The Light of the World*
Principal, New College, Edinburgh

NO INWARD VOCATION

No man ought to think of this profession, unless he feels within himself a love to religion, with a zeal for it, and an internal true piety, which is chiefly kept up by secret prayer, and by reading of the scriptures. As long as these things are a man's burdens, they are infallible indications, that he has no inward vocation, nor motion of the Holy Ghost to undertake it. The capital error in men's preparing themselves for that function is, that they study books more than themselves.

—Gilbert Burnet
(1643-1714)
The Conclusion
Minister at Saltoun; Bishop of Salisbury

October 8

TO BEAR THY PEOPLE

Wisdom and zeal and faith impart,
    Firmness with meekness, from above,
To bear Thy people on their heart,
    And love the souls whom Thou dost love;
To watch and pray, and never faint;
    By day and night strict guard to keep;
To warn the sinner, cheer the saint,
    Nourish Thy lambs, and feed Thy sheep.

—James Montgomery
(1771-1854)
Original Hymns
Moravian Minister; Poet; Missionary, West Indies

October 9

DISCIPLESHIP CARRIES AN OPTION

The method of getting people into relationship with God out of pity for Jesus is never recognised by our Lord. It does not put sin in its right place, nor does it put the Gospel in its right place. Our Lord never pressed anyone to follow Him unconditionally; nor did He wish to be followed merely out of an impulse of enthusiasm. He never pleaded, He never entrapped; He made discipleship intensely narrow, and pointed out certain things which could never be in those who followed Him. Today there is a tendency to take the harshness out of our Lord's statements. What Jesus says *is* hard; it is only easy when it comes to those who are His disciples. Whenever our Lord talked about discipleship He prefaced it with an "if," never with an emphatic assertion "you must." Discipleship carries an option with it.

—Oswald Chambers
(1874-1917)
Approved Unto God
Devotional Writer

150

BRANCH BEARS FOR ITS MASTER

And what is fruit? Something that the branch bears not for itself
but for its owner. Because Christians do not understand or
accept this truth, they fail so often in their efforts and prayers to
live the branch life. They desire it earnestly; they read and
meditate and pray, and yet they fail, and wonder why. The
reason is simple: they do not know that fruit-bearing is the one
thing for which they have been saved.

—Andrew Murray
(1828-1917)
Sermon: *The True Vine*
Minister and Devotional Writer, South Africa

GOD IS NEAR

Many live in this strange world, filled with tokens of a Divine
presence, just as if there were no real God. If in words they
admit His existence, they do not wish to have Him nigh at
hand.... To all who are so living I desire to reiterate, *God is
near*. He is near you *now;* yea, at the very door of your heart. He
has been near you in all your forgetfulness of Him, visiting you
with an unwearied loving-kindness and tender mercies. Take
advantage of that nearness.... Speak to Him at once; acknowledge your sin, tell Him all that is in your heart.

—James Culross
(1824-1899)
Sermon: *A Spiritual, All-Present
Personality*
Baptist Minister at Glasgow and Stirling

ARE YOU BEING CONVERTED?

You have had placed before you the signs of the absence of
conversion: habitual consent to known sin; willing resistance to
known and unpalatable truth; remembering past sin with
pleasure; delight in the society of the wicked; faint perceptions
of the difference between sins and sinfulness; insensibility to
sins of omission; and confidence in man's own light and
strength. Are you being converted?

—Alexander Penrose Forbes
(1817-1875)
A Commentary on the Litany
Bishop of Brechin

October 13

I NOW FORGAVE AND FORGOT

I look upon that as the time of my conversion, because of these considerations; First, because then and thereafter I found my heart wholly changed as to my friends and my favourites. I now felt a new delight in thinking of those men whom I believed to be true men of God. And men whom I simply hated before because of some real or supposed disobligement I had suffered àt their hands, I now forgave and forgot all that, and took them to my heart. I now found myself putting them in the right, and myself in the wrong. I now wished them and theirs all the good that was good for them. I remembered what John said about himself and the other apostles: "We know," he said, "that we have passed from death unto life, because we love the brethren." And as I read that I reasoned that the text which satisfied and assured the disciple whom Jesus loved might surely satisfy and assure me.

—Sir James Fraser of Brea
(1639-1699)
Memoirs of Himself
(While a student at Edinburgh University and aged 17)

October 14

NOT INSIGNIFICANT CYPHERS

We have work to do here...and finding that we have active natures, large capacities, and boundless cravings, can we think we are sent here to be idle? We are by no means assigned to be insignificant cyphers....God has given us a day in which we may do our work. We have life prolonged, offers and seasons of grace continued, God's patience waiting and His Spirit striving.... The Great Master will call us to an account what work we have done, and how we have done it. Should we set ourselves down, and examine ourselves what we have done of the work what a poor account should we bring in!

—Henry Davidson
(1687-1756)
Letters: *To Miss J.H.,
Edinburgh 10/10/1754*

Minister, Galashiels

WE ARE ... BUT CHRIST...

We cannot think of Him without being conscious of our need. We rejoice then to know that with the urgent sense of need, He brings the grace to supply it. For this is what His coming means: We are sinners, but Christ came into the world to save sinners. We are weak, but Christ's grace is open to us. We are tempted, but Christ is our strength. We have a hard duty to do, but Christ is by our side, and it can be done for His sake. We have death to meet some day, but Jesus lives. We have heaven and judgment to face, but He will stand with us in that day. Henceforth we shall seek Him, trust Him, follow Him; and they that follow Him shall not walk in darkness, but shall have the light of life.

—Edgar Primrose Dickie
(1897-   )
Christ or Chaos
Professor of Divinity, St. Andrews

IT IS ONLY BECAUSE...

If any Christian finds that his soul is not sufficiently raised above the down-dragging influence of earthly things, and his life not transformed, gradually but surely, into the beauty of holiness, it is only because he does not often enough climb the hill of secret communion with God, nor linger long enough there to catch its heavenly glow. We need to be much in the company of God if we are to understand God, to sympathise with God, to feel as God feels, to resemble God.

—George H. Knight
(D. 1937)
In the Secret of his Presence
Minister, Garelochhead

NO LIFE WITHOUT SCARS

I suppose there is no life which has not its scars; and there is nothing so precious and gracious if they be "marks of the Lord Jesus." You remember yon sacrifice which cut into your very heart, you were called in the providence of God to choose betwixt loss and honour, betwixt your own happiness and the duty which you owed to others, and you chose the nobler part. It cost you cruel anguish at the moment, and your life is maimed to this hour. But have you ever regretted that you made the sacrifice? that when you stood at the parting of the ways, you had the courage to take the steep and painful road, and shoulder your heavy cross. That was the crisis of your life, and there is never a day but you bless God for the choice you made. Your multilation is your gladness and your glory.

—David Smith
(1866-1932)
Sermon: *A Linen Cloth About Him*
Professor of Theology, Londonderry

A ROBE FOR SINNERS

God has provided a robe for guilty sinners, in which they may appear before Him without spot or blemish. It is the righteousness of Christ—of Him who is over all, God blessed for evermore; and who, to weave His wondrous web which was to clothe His people, left the throne of His glory; took on Him the form of a servant, and suffered and died upon the Cross, the just for the unjust. Arrayed in this robe, the believer is meet for the inheritance of the saints in light. All his iniquities are covered, his transgressions are forgiven....Nor is the robe merely an external covering; such is its virtue, that it penetrates and heals the soul of all who wear it.

—James Alexander Haldane
(1786-1851)
The Pharisee and the Publican
Independent evangelist

NO CONCEALING CRUST

I do most firmly believe, O anxious sinner, whomsoever you be, and whatsoever may have been your character, that all that Jesus did on Calvary He did for you....Jesus came into the world to save sinners....The word *sinners* in this blessed passage is no crust that conceals beneath it the word *the elect*. It is an honest word....It is as great as the world. What word is more universal than *sinner*?

> —James Morison
> (1816-1893)
> *The Extent of the Propitiation*
Minister of United Secession Church

GO DOWN TO THE DEPTHS

Cease your contentions as to forms of religion. Cease from the arrogance of your dry, logical speculations; give up frivolity or cynicism. Go down to the depths of your being in your hearts and consciences. Is there no divine voice speaking within? If there be, though it speak but in a whisper, be sure you listen to it. Think of the reality of things now as men think of them on their death-beds, and then I feel sure you will agree with David and St. Paul; you will feel and know you are a sinner, and this will stir you to help others who are sinners, who are sinners like yourself, but who are not sinners without hope, because Christ was born, was tempted, died, and rose, and lives now interceding that He may save them and you.

> —Archibald Campbell Tait
> (1811-1882)
> Sermon: *The Prevalence of Sin*
Archbishop of Canterbury

BECAUSE YOU ARE SINFUL

We make our sin an argument for fearing God. He makes it an argument for coming nigh. The utmost we can think of Him as saying is, "*Although* you are sinful, you may come." *He* puts it another way, "*Because* you are sinful, come—come because you need me so much." Alas for all of us, if we needed to stop sinning before we could confidently pray! Alas for us if only perfect men could come boldly to the Throne of Grace! If we go to God at all, we must, like the prodigal, go in our rags, and hunger, and sin, and utter need: but the compassionate Father, whose heart has never changed, will see us while we are yet 'a great way off'—for He has been on the outlook for us, waiting for our coming—and He will shorten the distance between us and Him by going forth to meet us.

> —George H. Knight
> (D. 1937)
> Sermon: *When Alone With God*

Minister, Garelochhead

GOD HAS PLACED CHRIST

I am not here today to tell you only that you are a sinner, vile, and helpless—an outcast. This is not all my message. That I leave to your conscience and the open Bible before you....Do not plead your inability and your wickedness. That is but an excuse for delay....Sinner, the Lord bids me tell you this day that He has placed Christ within your reach in the Gospel.... He will give you a heart to love Him and strength to follow Him wheresoever He leads.

> —John Kennedy
> (1819-1884)
> Sermon: *The White-robed Multitude*

Minister, Dingwall

THE LAST BLOOD SHED

"There remaineth now no more sacrifice for sin." "Without shedding of blood there is no remission." God help you if you reject the Cross! There was shed the last blood that ever shall be shed for human sin.

> —John McNeill
> (1854-1933)
> *Sermon*

Evangelist and Minister

SUBTRACTING THE DIVINE LOVE

The Atonement...was the Divine Love struggling against the habit of sin, the law of retribution, the demands of justice. It was like the sun's rays, its light and heat, breaking through cloud and mist, and turning them into shapes of beauty and glory. There was a power warmth and brightness in the Divine Love to change the dampness and darkness of sin into repentance and regenerated life. You may as well try to understand and admire a sunset, subtracting the sun, as to understand the Atonement, subtracting the Divine Love.

—John F. Ewing
(1849-1890)
Sermon: *The Atonement*
Minister, Toorak, Melbourne, Australia

THAT IS THE ATONING SACRIFICE

What keeps the whole idea of the forgiveness of sins sound and wholesome is the Christian Gospel of the divine atoning sacrifice. If we hold that Cross of Christ before our eyes, then we shall never make the divine forgiveness either too cheap on the one hand or too impossible on the other. Some make it too cheap and easy, as if our sins did not matter much; and that is not the way to better things. Others make it too difficult, and can't forgive themselves at all, and that also is not the way to better things. But we can't make the first mistake if we remember what our sins have done to the Son of God. And we can't make the second mistake if we remember what the Son of God has done with our sins. And these two things come together in the Cross of Christ. That is the Atoning Sacrifice.

—Donald Macpherson Baillie
(1887-1954)
The Atoning Sacrifice
Professor of Theology, St. Andrews

IT IS NOT INTERESTING IF...

This doctrine (Atonement) is ineffective and indeed uninterest-ing mainly for two reasons.... It is not interesting if we are *not* seriously interested in sin. If sin is regarded with comparative indifference—if it is treated as a slight or superficial matter which we can deal with for ourselves... if we have never learned the power of the bad conscience to paralyse the will—then of course the atonement will seem gratuitous to us and we will not get experience of its cleansing power. And on the other hand, it is not interesting, if we *are* really interested in sin. The man who has been compromised with evil and who, for reasons of his own, intends to continue so—this man can have nothing to do with the atonement.

—James Denney
(1856-1917)
To His Students
Professor of Theology, Glasgow

SOLITUDE SPEAKS TO US

And thus the loneliness that drops down upon the sinner is one of God's mercies after all. When a light goes suddenly out, we look round startled by what is happening; we begin to think, and feel for something that will turn the light up again; and just so the wretched isolation of guilt is God's call to us and God's opportunity. He sets us apart in misery in order that we may call upon Him. He puts us utterly by ourselves that we may become more sensitive to the hand that is touching us in the darkness. He shuts us in that we may have no choice but to think of Him. The solitude speaks to us. We can hear what it is saying, and as we listen the message shapes itself into a promise: "Thou hast destroyed thyself, but in Me is thine help."

—Hugh Ross Mackintosh
(1870-1936)
Sermon: *Solitude and Faith*
Professor of Systematic Theology, Edinburgh

MYSTERIES REMAIN BUT...

It is no part of the Christian Faith that mystery is banished from the world. The Christian doctrine affirms that we know *in part* and see as in the baffling reflections of a mirror. Mysteries remain, but to those who hold the Faith, that is, to those who are humble enough in mind to allow themselves to be told the Good News of Jesus, they are now mysteries of light and not of darkness. And that is true even of the final mysteries of suffering and death.

—Sir Thomas Murray Taylor
(1897-1962)
Sermon: *The House Filled With Smoke*

Professor of Law; Principal, Aberdeen University

THE ONE COMFORT TO US

How beautiful the separation made by death!—We cannot learn from the dead what they have gone through, and what they have seen. Every one of us must pass through that gate. The one comfort to us is that the purpose of Him who made us is certainty that we should be righteous—partakers of His own righteousness, and of His own blessedness. We cannot reasonably doubt this. And if this is to be His desire and purpose for us all, can we believe that He will ever give it up? Impossible.... The love of God in the spiritual is like the centre of gravity in the material world, which not only attracts all things to itself, but unites them harmoniously to each other.

—Thomas Erskine of Linlathen
(1788-1870)
Letters—*To Lady Caroline Charteris*

Legal Authority and Theologian

HE IS EQUALLY THE SAME

God, seen as our Father, makes all things sweet, all paths straight, reconciles all things. This Fatherhood, once truly accepted, solves all perplexities, and makes the difficulties of life clear and plain. He is our Father, and, whatever is meant by that name, that He is, and always so. Life, death, make no alteration in this relationship. In life, after death, He is equally the same, and Father. Beyond the shores of death we do not go into a strange country; it is still our Father's house, where the Father is dealing with His children as they require. No time, no space, can destroy His eternal, uniform, and paternal relation.

—Alexander Ewing
(1814-1873)
Sermon

Bishop of Argyll and Isles

THE ABODE OF CHARITY

But death shall be destroyed at last: and there is a resurrection; and there is a judgment to come. Then the veil of ignorance shall be taken away: and the arts of wilful misrepresentation shall be exposed: and the sentence of truth shall be pronounced: and that mercy will be experienced from God, which is here denied by man. Heaven is the abode of charity; and there all our contentions shall be forgotten: and united in the bonds of everlasting love, we shall join together in the grateful, and harmonious and never-ending song of praise, to Him whose kindness has never forsaken us, and who has provided 'a rest for the people of God.'

—Andrew Thomson
(1779-1831)
Sermon: *Views on Death*

Minister, St. George's, Edinburgh

BY DEATH'S DARK STILE

Carry me over the long last mile,
    Man of Nazareth, Christ for me!
Weary I wait by Death's dark stile,
    In the wild and the waste, where the wind blows free;
And the shadows and sorrows come out of my past,
    Look clean through my heart,
    And will not depart,
Now that my poor world has come to its last.

Lord, is it long that my spirit must wait?
    Man of Nazareth, Christ for me!
Deep is the stream, and the night is late,
    And grief blinds my soul that I cannot see.
Speak to me out of the silences, Lord,
    That my spirit may know
    As forward I go,
Thy pierc'd hands are lifting me over the ford.

            —Lauchlan MacLean Watt
            (1867-1957)

Preacher and Poet

MEET DEATH WITH JOY

Make sure of an interest in the precious sacrifice and the meritorious passion of Jesus. In his righteousness you can meet death with joy. Through Him you will be more than conqueror. Death has no advantage whether he comes as a friend or as a foe, for in the one capacity you are prepared to welcome him, and in the other to vanquish him. It is only when death comes as a stranger, that his stroke is dreadful. By you, I trust, he is duly estimated—stingless, sinless, curseless, because to you Christ is precious—the eternal Spirit, your comforter, the everlasting God, your Father, and unutterable glory your home.

            —John Cumming
            (1807-1881)
            Sermon: *The House Appointed*
            for All Living
Minister, Crown Court, London

ON SECRET FOREIGN SERVICE

There are those who can quietly say, as their faith follows their love into the unseen, "I know that land. Some of my people live there. Some have gone there on secret foreign service, which does not admit of communications. But I meet from time to time the Commanding Officer. And when I mention them to Him He assures me all is well."

—Peter Taylor Forsyth
(1848-1921)
This Life and the Next
Preacher, Theologian, Writer

HE SENDS NO ANGELS NOW

This, too, I believe, that the gracious Friend of man is very near to us in our passage from this world to another. He sends no angels now, but comes close to us Himself, by a true personal access, and fulfils His Word. "I will come and take you to Myself, that where I am, there ye may be also." When our dearest earthly friends fall back He steps forward and takes up the fainting thread of thought and feeling, and carries it on to the life beyond.

—John Ker
(1819-1886)
Letters—1866-85
Preacher

I SHALL SLEEP IN CHRIST

I shall sleep in Christ, and when I awake I shall be satisfied with His likeness. O for a well-tuned harp! There is nothing now between me and the Resurrection but 'this day thou shalt be with me in Paradise.' Glory, glory dwelleth, in Immanuel's land.

—Samuel Rutherford
(1600-1661)
(Dying Words: March 30, 1661)
Preacher and Devotional Writer, St. Andrews

NOW SET ME FREE

O Lord my God, I have hoped in Thee,
    Jesus beloved, now set me free.
In harshest chain, in wretched pain,
    In weakness and in sorrow sore,
Upon my knees and at my prayers
    I beg Thee that Thou freest me.

> —Mary, Queen of Scots
> (1542-1587)
> (Written before her execution)

Rough translation of the Latin:

O Domine Deus, speravi in te!
O care mi Jesu, nunc libera me!
In dura catena, in misera poena,
Languende, gemende, et genu flectende,
Adore, implore, ut liberes me!

THESE ARE BRAVE GIFTS

I shall be in heaven shortly; I shall come there by the word of my testimony and the blood of the Lamb. All is of grace. He has chosen me, called me, justified me, and sanctified me by His grace. He gives grace and glory. These are brave gifts....(He died crying) Free grace! Free grace!

> —Thomas Halyburton
> (1674-1712)
> (On his deathbed)

MAKE SURE WE HAVE GOT IT!

Now what is it to lay hold on eternal life? It is to do exactly what we would do in the case of some earthly treasure, *make sure* we have got it. Let us give no sleep to our eyes, nor slumber to our eyelids, till we have grasped the hand which is stretched out to us, waiting for us to put forth ours to take hold of it. Let us remember for our encouragement that this is all that is needed. Our part alone remains unfinished. His hand is stretched out still!

> —Lady Grisell Baillie
> (1822-1891)
> *Fight the Good Fight*

Devotional Writer; First Deaconess of the Church of Scotland

JUST GROUNDS TO SING

As to the state of my health I have just grounds to sing of mercy and of judgment; since you was in this place, I have had nothing of the racking pains, only the pain of my breast doth frequently give me uneasiness, but it is sufferable. What reason I have to adore sovereign goodness, and to set a seal to that truth of his being the prayer-hearing God. May I get grace to be more humble, fruitful and watchful.

—Henry Davidson
(1687-1756)
Letter: January 10, 1732

Minister, Galashiels

THANK THEE FOR MY THORN

My God, I have never thanked Thee for my thorn. I have thanked Thee a thousand times for my roses, but never once for my thorn. I have been looking forward to a world where I shall get compensation for my cross, but I have never thought of my cross itself as a present glory. Teach me the glory of my cross. Teach me the value of my thorn. Show me that I have climbed to Thee by the path of pain. Show me that my tears have been my rainbow.

—George Matheson
(1842-1906)

Preacher and Poet

GOD AND MAN TOUCH

Trial brings man face to face with God—God and he touch; and the flimsy veil of bright cloud that hung between him and the sky is blown away; he feels that he is standing outside the earth with nothing between him and the Eternal Infinite. Oh! there is something in the sick-bed, and the aching heart, and the restlessness and the langour of shattered health, and the sorrow of affections withered, and the stream of life poisoned at its fountain, and the cold, lonely feeling of utter rawness of heart which is felt when God strikes home in earnest, that forces a man to feel what is real and what is not.

> —Frederick William Robertson
> (1816-1853)
> Sermon: *Realising the Second Advent*

Minister, Trinity Chapel, Brighton

THIS EVER-PRESENT LOAD

Sooner or later—and to some it comes very early—there is a trouble or sorrow that is always there. It may be some weakness of body, some ever-present pain, some oft-recurring sickness. It may be the remembrance of a frustrated ambition, some disappointed hope, some buried love, or, worse than all, the remembrance of a very bitter day in life—of sin that has been repented of—or even sin of others unrepented of. There is this ever-present load. We have fresh sorrows now and again, the illnesses that mark our years, little harvests of pain, but underneath and over all there is always some root of bitterness. And God will not remove it. We pray thrice like Paul—aye, or three hundred times, and the trouble remains.... Paul got more than he sought—"Grace," which means "gift." God's gifts are part of Himself. "My grace is sufficient for thee."

> —John Paterson Struthers
> (1851-1915)
> Sermon: *Paul's Unanswered Prayer*

Minister; Publisher, Greenock

GOD COMES ... AND BIDS

How difficult it is to believe, yet how true it is, that Christ is nearest to us when we feel our hearts most paralysed, and the very heavens cold and silent over us! In the momentary paroxysm of human grief, our eyes are often holden that we do not see Him who comes to show us how fruitful suffering can be. For it is shared by a God, not once for all set up in solitary glory, "calmly contented with what He has done," but by a God who "in all our afflictions is afflicted." The Cross is not gone: it has only removed from Calvary to within the heart of God. In "fiery pangs on battlefields, on fevered beds where sick men toss"; in the pathos of blotted-out horizons; in every swift blow of bereavement, where the fire of our heart is turned to ashes; and in the refined agony of hope deferred, God comes to us in the healing Christ and bids us to be of good cheer.

—George B. Burnet
(1894-   )
Sermon: *The Sacred Heart*
Minister of Corsock, Castle Douglas

PESSIMISM IS HEARTLESS

If a man desires to be young in his soul let him receive the spirit of Jesus, and bathe his soul in the Christian hope. Ah, pessimism is a heartless, helpless spirit. If one despairs of the future for himself and for his fellows, then he had better die at once. It is despair which cuts the sinews of a man's strength and leaves him at the mercy of temptations.

—John Watson
(1850-1907)
Sermon: *Humanity's Golden Age*
Pastor and Professor

FOREIGN TO CHRIST

That tired, apathetic, beaten feeling that steals over us at times, that faithless conclusion that there is no use trying further, that things are far too dour and crabbed ever to be straightened out, but must remain much as they are, is foreign to Christ. We allow ourselves to be tamed by life, grow broken, unexpectant, disillusioned, drift with the times as being the only thing that we can do. But He feels that in the same world with God anything may happen; and He will set no limit to what may be.... Boldly He goes to the most hopeless-looking and impossible people and startles them out of themselves into a better life by the sheer daring of His hopes for them, and the glory of His faith in them, and the audacity of His unquestioning belief in the hugeness of what He is quite sure they are prepared to give and do.

—Arthur John Gossip
(1873-1954)
Sermon: *The Galilean Accent*
Preacher and Professor, Trinity College, Glasgow

November 16

LET US ENCOURAGE OURSELVES

Why should we entertain such unreasonable fears, which dampen our spirits, and weaken our hands, and augment the difficulties of our way? Let us encourage ourselves with those mighty aids we are to expect in this spiritual welfare; for greater is he that is for us, than all that can rise up against us: "The eternal God is our refuge" (Deuteronomy 33:27), "and underneath are the everlasting arms," "Let us be strong in the Lord, and in the power of his might" (Ephesians 6:10), for he it is that shall "tread down our enemies" (Psalm 44:5).

—Henry Scougal
(1650-1678)
The Life of God in the Soul of Man
Professor of Theology; Bishop of Aberdeen

BE ASHAMED OF PESSIMISM

The Christian must be saved by Hope. He must face the rough
weather of the world, fearless and undismayed. He must be
ashamed of pessimism, just as a soldier must be afraid of
cowardice upon the battle field. He must live his life by the
supernatural virtues of Faith and Hope and Love which lead
men on the Everlasting Way. The Faith which is very sure that
by the great act of the incarnation God has joined His life and
fortunes to our fortunes and our life by bands that neither
Death nor Hell can break. The Love which constrains us to
look always on our fellow men with the invincible loyalty of
Him whose great heart never faltered not even when they
crucified His love. The Hope which even in the darkest night
can look upward with gay confidence to the shining of the stars.

—Frederick Llewellyn Deane
(1868-1952)
Sermon: *Christ and the Pessimist*

Bishop of Aberdeen

TO BE TRULY HAPPY

To be truly happy is a question of how we begin and not on how
we end, of what we want and not of what we have. An
aspiration is a joy for ever, a possession as solid as a landed
estate, a fortune which we can never exhaust and which gives us
year by year a revenue of pleasurable activity. To have many of
these is to be spiritually rich. Life is only a very dull and ill-
directed theatre unless we have some interests in the piece; and
to those who have neither art nor science, the world is a mere
arrangement of colours, or a rough footway where they may
very well break their shins. It is in virtue of his own desires and
curiosities that any man continues to exist even with patience,
that he is charmed by the look of things and people, and that he
wakens every morning with a renewed appetite for work and
pleasure.

—Robert Louis Stevenson
(1850-1894)
El Dorado

Writer and Poet

THE ONLY HAPPINESS AND GOODNESS

I suppose that all of us want to be happy and some of us, perhaps, want to be good, but happiness and goodness are not the things that can be manufactured for us either by our fellow men, or even by God. Yet people often talk as though they could. The only happiness that is really happy, and the only goodness that is really good, is the kind that we ourselves have had a hand in creating; by doing our duty, by loving our neighbours, by patience and courage, and kindness, and loyalty, by excellence in work, by playing the man, by doing our best under difficult circumstances, by carrying our Cross.

—George Matheson
(1842-1906)
Moments on the Mount
Preacher and Poet

HE IS THE FOOD

When we say, Give us this day our daily bread, we say, "Give eternal things, give the things of time. Thou hast promised us a kingdom, give us the means of attaining it. Thou wilt give us eternal glory with Thyself, give us for the time support on earth."... Christ is ... the food which refresheth yet faileth not, which is received not yet consumed, which satisfieth the longing soul, yet remaineth entire. He is the food which supports us in our weary pilgrimage here below, gladdening us by the anticipation of the future joys of glory; He is the food of angels, and the everlasting delight of the saints, in which may we in the end have a share; and we shall have a share therein according to His promise, if only we walk humbly with our God, if only we covet the best things, if only we wean ourselves from the world, and ever desire this daily bread.

—Alexander Penrose Forbes
(1817-1875)
A Commentary on the Litany
Bishop of Brechin

NOT DISPOSERS OF OUR OWN LOT

We are not disposers of our own lot; the Father of spirits has perfect control of those spiritual processes within us that affect us so deeply and may change us so radically. In many an unwilling breast there stirs a movement toward spiritual realities which we cannot control. We may resist and oppose it and try to stem it, but we shall find it as irresistable as the wind, since it is the moving of the life-giving Spirit of God.

—Roderick A. Finlayson
(1895-   )
Sermon: *The Wind of the Spirit*
Professor, Free Church College, Edinburgh

THE DREAM OF THE SPIRIT

Under the burden of sin, and the felt discordance in our being, the soul of man cries out for the living God. The dream of the spirit is to be delivered from its weakness and unrest, from imprisonment in its present bonds, into a purer and fuller life, in which its haunting visions of holiness and peace and self control shall come true, and achievement, no longer baffled by a recreant will and halting energies, shall follow hard on aspiration. That ideal has been realised in Christ.

—Daniel John Ferguson
(1845-1886)
Sermon: *Law and Miracle*
Minister at Strathbane

HAVING DONE ALL—HE STOOD

That this grand and passionate nature should be turned into a loving, working, quiet power; that through the years he did not yield to dismay or bitterness; was not tempted by base compliance; was not elated by passing victories; that, having done all, he stood—such was the triumph of St. Paul. It is the triumph of all saints. We glory most not in their brilliant and victorious hours, but in their steadfast perseverance through light and shadow to the end.

—William Robertson Nicoll
(1851-1923)
Sermon: *The Seen and the Unseen*
Preacher, Publisher, Writer

MY INTEREST AND HIS TRUTH

This is the most joyful day that ever I saw in my pilgrimage on earth. My joy is now begun, which I see shall never be interrupted. I see both my interest and His truth, and the sureness of the one, and the preciousness of the other. It is near thirty years since He made it sure; and since that time, though there has fallen out much sin, yet I was never out of an assurance of mine interest, nor long out of sight of His presence. He has dandled me, and kept me lively, and never left me behind, though I was ofttimes turning back. Oh! He has showed the wonderful preciousness of His grace, not only in the first receiving thereof, but in renewed and multiplied pardons! I have been a man of great sins, but He has been a God of great mercies; and now, through His mercies, I have a conscience as sound and quiet as if I had never sinned.

—Donald Cargill
(1619-1681)
Testimony at His Execution
Minister, Barony, Glasgow; Covenanting Martyr

WHAT DEFENCE, WHAT SUPPORT

And now, you followers of Jesus, what defence, what support, what guidance can you need, which this your king, who is God Almighty, cannot afford you—which this your ruler, who is love, will not supply? In all your frailties and ignorances and temptations manifold, remember that your Divine Sovereign is man, and has suffered being tempted, and is qualified to succour you when you are tempted. Be not startled by dangers, nor scared by enemies; neither faint at the thought of your own weakness, and the power of the devil, and his cunning, and the cruel malice of his servants. Let the almightiness and infinite love of your most gracious King, God's son, assure your hearts, that following him, you shall be conquerors, yea more than conquerors.

—Robert Lee
(1804-1868)
Sermon: *The Incarnation*
Minister, Old Greyfriars, Edinburgh

BE TRULY THANKFUL

If you are spiritually alive through Jesus Christ the bread of life, be truly thankful and express the gratitude of your heart in the obedience of your life. While you look to the past with gratitude, contemplate the future with confidence. You are as dependent as ever, but Christ is as able and willing as ever to give you supply. You are not straitened in Him: be not straitened in yourselves. Use the means which He has himself appointed, and His blessing shall not be denied you. Be not content to *have* life, seek to enjoy it.

—David Crawford
(1794-1865)
Sermon: *Christ the Bread of Life*
Minister, United Presbyterian Church, Edinburgh

A CAPITAL CRIME

Alas! for the capital crime of the Lord's people—barrenness of praises. O, how fully I am persuaded that a line of praises is worth a leaf of prayer, and an hour of praises is worth a day of fasting and mourning!

—John Livingston
(1603-1672)
Letter to a Friend
Minister at Ancrum; Exiled to Rotterdam

TO DECLARE AND WITNESS

O Lord, the blind dullness of our corrupt nature will not suffer us sufficiently to weight these Thy most ample benefits; yet, nevertheless, at the commandment of Jesus Christ our Lord, we present ourselves to this His Table to declare and witness before the world that by Him alone we have entrance to the throne of Thy grace; that by Him alone we are possessed in our spiritual kingdom, to eat and drink at His Table.... And these most inestimable benefits we acknowledge and confess to have received of Thy free mercy and grace, by Thy only beloved Son Jesus Christ.

—John Knox
(1505-1572)
Prayer at Lord's Supper
Reformer; Minister at St. Giles, Edinburgh

172

SO APPARENT, SO URGENT

May the faithfulness, the utterness of Christ's devotion come down on us! May His love consume in us all that is dishonourable, break the bands that bind us to sin, engage everyone of our faculties, and bring us with every talent we possess and every opportunity to the service of God and His kingdom....May every one of us be moved today by these mercies of God—so apparent, so urgent, to present our bodies a living sacrifice, holy and acceptable unto God, which is our reasonable service.

—George Adam Smith
(1858-1942)
Sermon: *Before Communion*
Semitic Scholar; Principal, Aberdeen University

WHAT SAY YOU TO THAT?

Perhaps there is some trembling, weak believer here, that is doubting whether he has grace or not, and fearing he has no interest in the Man that is God's Fellow. Tell me, will you quit your past in Him? Could you freely choose to take the world and your lusts, and let others take Christ who please? Would you find in your heart to rest contented with other things, and give to anybody your part in Christ? Why say you to that, poor, doubting soul?

—Ralph Erskine
(1685-1752)
Communion Address
Preacher, Burgher (Secession Church)

DAYSPRING FROM ON HIGH

This is the visit of the dayspring from on high, in his actual incarnation or manifestation in our nature. This was the rising of the sun in the open view of the world. O how did this Sun of righteousness rejoice to run his race of humiliation in this lower world, having his divine glory obscured with a veil of flesh, lest his dazzling glory should have overwhelmed us. By this one visit he fulfilled the law, satisfied justice, finished transgression, made an end of sin, brought in everlasting righteousness, confirmed the covenant, overthrew principalities and powers, destroyed death, opened up the way to the holy and earth, by which God might come to man without prejudice to his justice, and man might come unto God without being consumed or overwhelmed.

—Ebenezer Erskine
(1680-1754)
The Dayspring From on High

Clergyman

EVERY DAY PRESENTING HIMSELF

Would you be prepared for Christ's second appearance, my brothers, be at pains to make yourself acquainted with Him beforehand. He is every day presenting Himself to you, in the works of His hands—His sun rises day by day to light you to His service, and to measure the distance from eternity, that is diminishing with amazing rapidity. His voice speaks to you sometimes in the soft murmur of the zephyr, now in the roar of the whirlwind, and at other times in the bellowing thunder— His meekness breathes in the spring, His glory blazes in the summer, His bounty swells in the harvest, and His terrors appal in the winter.... What object is there, O Christian, in nature, in providence, or in grace wherein we do not behold the name of Jesus the Lord, written in great characters?

—Henry Hunter
(1741-1802)
The Coming of Jesus

Minister, Scots Church, London Wall

174

OUR ULTIMATE GOAL OF LIFE

Fellowship with Christ in the light of God is the only possible way in which we can conceive the ultimate goal of the life of our spirits. Hence, we must hold to the spiritual aspect of the Second Coming, whether or not we can make other assertions about it. We feel, with one of the New Testament writers, that in many respects the nature of the Life Hereafter has not been revealed, but equally we must feel with him the certainty that that Life can only be conceived in terms of spiritual likeness to Christ: "We know that, when we shall be manifested, we shall be like Him, for we shall see Him as He is."

—William Manson
(1882-1958)
Asking Them Questions
Professor of New Testament, Edinburgh

SWINGS THE CHAIN OF HISTORY

We have a double witness to bear in this as in every generation. One half of the witness stretches backward to the Cross and proclaims—"Christ has come": the other reaches onward to the Throne and proclaims—"Christ will come." Between these two high uplifted piers swings the chain of the world's history.

—Alexander McLaren
(1826-1922)
Minister

WHEN JESUS SHALL RETURN

At the same time, long for the hour when Jesus shall return to lift up, and repair, and ennoble all that was thrown down on the day of our fall. The curse is on all things as yet—and what if it should press still more heavily, as we draw nearer the close of this dispensation? Ah! the shadows of evening do steal quickly over us. Light after light goes out in our aged firmament. Beneath our feet all foundations tremble, and the travail of the earth is great. But, just as in the sorer travail of Calvary, when the darkness was at its height, a voice is suddenly heard out of the heavenly temple, crying, *"It is done!"* The crisis is over. Now breaks forth the restrained Sun, and the darkness flees. The archangel's trumpet wakes up the sainted dead, the living, too, are changed. The old veil of time is rent in twain. And, from the holy place of the Church below, we pass into the holiest of all—*there,* amid hosannahs, to receive from the Last Adam, "the wisdom," and "the might," and "the riches," we lost in the first.

—John James Bonar
(1803-1891)

Minister, Greenock

AGNOSTICISM ... MAY BE DUE TO ...

Agnosticism has many causes. It may have its roots in genuine perplexity as to the difficult problems set by the universe to the thinking mind. Or it may be due to an unwillingness to surrender our lives completely to what we know to be best. In that case, owing to well-known psychological laws, the mind emits a mist which hides or discolours all the heavens and prevents us from seeing the sun in his strength. Or it may be due, as I have said, to moral revolt against a traditional theology, to which one sees no alternative except the denial that such a God exists. Or it may be all three together!

Atheism is a pathological condition of the human spirit, and agnosticism is a confession that we are beaten! Both are profoundly unsatisfactory states of consciousness for any one who desires to keep his soul alive and to "overcome the world."

—David Smith Cairns
(1862-1946)
What Is Salvation?

Principal, Christ's College, Aberdeen

CHRIST HIMSELF BRINGS FAITH

It is with the heart that man believeth unto righteousness. Disbelief is always a thing chiefly of the heart. Some sudden shake has deranged that delicate organ; some loss has paralysed it, frozen it into stone; some of its longings have failed to be supplied, or its aspirations, like smoking flax, have been rudely stamped upon and quenched. Then...we lay the blame of our infidelity on some outside thing—want of evidence, the contradictions in Revelation, the scandalous life of Christians. Could we but see this question answered reasonably, or this contradiction reconciled honestly, or this seeming immorality or cruelty ascribed openly to God, explained satisfactorily, we should believe. There are thousands to whom these things present no difficulty, who will not believe; and there are thousands to whom they are tremendous anxieties, who nevertheless believe with all the firmness their natures are capable of....It is Christ Himself, not the evidence of Him—it is Himself that brings faith. Thomas sought a sight of the wounds; he wished to read the Evidences. Christ Himself came, and superseded all that. Even so, come Lord Jesus.

—Andrew Bruce Davidson
(1831-1902)
Sermon: *On Thomas*
Professor of Theology, Glasgow

DOUBT - HONEST: OBSTINATE

Christ never failed to distinguish between doubt and unbelief. Doubt is *can't believe;* unbelief is *won't believe.* Doubt is honesty; unbelief is obstinacy. Doubt is looking for light; unbelief in contact with darkness. Loving darkness rather than light — that is what Christ attacked unsparingly. But for the intellectual questioning of Thomas, and Philip, and Nicodemus, and the many others who came to Him to have their great problems solved, He was respectful and generous and tolerant. How did Christ meet their doubts? He destroyed by fulfilling. When Thomas came to Him and denied His very resurrection, and stood before Him waiting for some scathing words and lashing for his unbelief, they never came. Christ gave him the facts. He said, "Behold My hands and My feet." He founded His religion upon facts. That is the great lesson of the New Testament way of looking at doubt — of Christ's treatment of doubt. It is not "Brand him": — but lovingly, wisely and tenderly to teach him. Faith is never opposed to reason in the New Testament; it is opposed to sight.

—Henry Drummond
(1851-1897)
Sermon: *Stones Rolled Away* 177
Writer and Lecturer

DOUBTS AND DENIALS

It has been my lot to be constantly involved in discussion with men who feel unable to identify themselves with the faith and outlook of the Christian Church, and it is seldom, if ever, that I have felt that their doubts and denials were based on a true understanding of what they were doubting and denying. Men criticise and oppose Christianity without ever taking much trouble to discover what it is all about.

—John Baillie
(1886-1960)
Invitation to Pilgrimage
Professor of Theology, Edinburgh

DOUBT AND DOUBT

There is doubt and doubt. There is doubt which springs from moral perversity, and doubt which springs from the desire to know the truth and to be true: the downward doubt and the upward; that which the baser minded enjoy, and that which pains the sincere. Christ had nothing to say to the former; but to the latter, in which reason is in conflict with the higher and uncorrupted instincts, He proffers His assistance. To the Scribes and Pharisees He did not and could not, manifest Himself. They had disqualified themselves by their moral aversion and by their spiritual apathy. What evidence could satisfy the reason when the heart refused to make the venture of love in answer to love? To Thomas, on the other hand, who was seeking to doubt himself into faith, He offered such satisfaction as the inquiring mind demanded.

—William Dickie
(1854-1935)
The Significance of Doubt
Minister, Dowanhill, Glasgow

WHY BE FAITHLESS OR DOUBTING?

Why should I, who have been the child of so many mercies, be faithless or doubting? If any man living should trust in the Lord absolutely and cast upon Him the burden of his cares, I am that man. All my days I have been a child of Providence, the Lord leading me and guiding me in ways unknown to me — in ways of His own, and for the accomplishment of His own heavenly ends. Oh, that I were more worthy! But, somehow, I feel as if the more marvellous the Lord's dealings with me, the more cold, heartless and indifferent I become. Is this not sad?—is it not terrible?...O Lord, soften, break, melt this hard heart of mine!

> —Alexander Duff
> (1806-1878)
> *Letter to his daughter*

Missionary to India

WHY I BELIEVE

Belief in God is not a human creation of a man's own powers; it is not a grace, which a man manufactures out of his own goodness or his ability to reason deeply. Belief in God is something which a man accepts from God, when he is willing so to do. It is a gift of God to men and women who will receive it. Belief is of all depths, from shallow to fathomless, and the deeper it is, the more worthy. Faith is a working of God within us, when we allow Him; its enemies are the pride which thinks it knows and the folly which imagines that faith can be done without. The soul which keeps looking up to God has already accepted the gift of God, which is faith, and knows, increasingly, its strength and light and comfort. "They looked unto him and were lightened," said the Psalmist of such as believe, "and their faces were not ashamed." That just about expresses why I believe.

> —James Hutchison Cockburn
> (1882-1973)
> *Why I Believe*

Minister, Dunblane Cathedral

CHRIST'S VIEW OF THE INTELLECT

There may have been things which Jesus Christ belittled but the intelligence of men was not among them. He never dreamed it would answer every question, but He recognised to the full its place and power, and breathed on it a new and ampler life.... But when in the richest and deepest gospel you hear the Saviour saying, "I am the truth," you hear Him claiming to be the Lord of the intellect, no less that the Redeemer of the soul. The way in which Jesus used that word gives us an insight into His view of the intellect. The Christian intellect must work in harmony with the whole Christian character. The mark of a Christian is not mental brilliance; it is an intellect which so ennobles character that heart and will and passion and intelligence unite together to the praise of God. You will never think rightly if you are living wrongly. Impure passions mean an untrue intellect.

—George H. Morrison
(1866-1928)
Sermon: *The Wings of the Morning*
Minister, Wellington, Glasgow

A SERVANT BY OBLIGATION

The well of living water which is planted in every individual heart the moment it is inspired and taken possession of by the Holy Spirit of God, does not increase its water and augment its volume by remaining still; on the contrary, the more it wells up and pours forth in multitudinous rivulets upon this world's deserts, the more it draws from its parent depths of everlasting life. He that is made a saint by grace, will instantly become a servant by obligation; and the evidence, the greatest, brightest, evidence of his saintship, are the toils and sacrifices of his service to men for Christ's sake.

—John Cumming
(1807-1881)
Sermon: *The Christian Religion
or No Religion*
Minister, Crown Court, London

HONOURED TO SUFFER ANY THING

My dear heart, bless the Lord on my behalf, that ever it should hav pleased such a holy God to hav looked upon such an unworthy sinner as I am, or to hav honoured the like of me to suffer any thing for His name's saik, or bear His cross in a day when ther is so few longing to wear His livery.... The Lord has made all things easy to me and He has been soe kind to my soul somtymes since I came to prison, that I hav counted all things nothing in comparison of Him.... *Now,* my dear, ye are dear, indeed, to me, bot not soe dear as Christ.

—Janet Lintoun
Letter to her husband
Covenanter imprisoned in Dunnottar Castle, 1684

LIVING ON A SLOPE

The Christianity which is not always pioneering in the sphere of the impossible will soon be rejected as mere lumber, useless to all but leisured minds. Where Christ ceases to be a challenge to our conscience in every direction, He will soon cease to be any kind of comfort to our hearts. The heart of a man has no use for a religion which can be domesticated like a tame cat, or a God who can be reduced to the level of an indulgent parent. We are living spiritually on a kind of slope, in which there is no alternative between the fight to move upwards and the slackness that drifts downwards. God quickens us into the hunger and thirst after righteousness! It is the only assurance we can have that we are alive.

—James Reid
(1887-1963)
The Key to the Kingdom
Minister, Eastbourne, England

181

HE CLAIMS POSSESSION

All earthly masters stand on one side, and He on the other, unique, alone, adequate, and infinite. And this being true, He claims, and has a right to claim, His place "in the midst" of your life and mine. We may not offer Him a place somewhere on the circumference. If He comes at all He will be central, the characterising and determining fact of your life. He wants to take possession of our whole nature, to pervade our whole being, to interpenetrate all our spirits, to draw us from the external and temporal, and by making His home in us to give us a home in the Divine and Eternal. Is He "in the midst" of your life, your business, your recreation, your friendships, your reading, your all? If so, heaven is not a distant prospect, but a present experience.

—William Graham Scroggie
(1877-1958)
Sermon: *Jesus in the Midst*
Baptist Minister, Charlotte Chapel, Edinburgh;
Principal, Spurgeon's College

TRUE RELIGION IS A UNION

So few understand what it [religion] means; some place in it the understanding, in orthodox notions and opinions; and all the account they can give of their religion is that they are of this or the other persuasion, and have joined themselves to one of those many sects whereinto Christendom is most unhappily divided. Others place it in the outward man, in a constant course of external duties and a model of performances.... Others again put all religion in the affections, in rapturous hearts and ecstatic devotion.... They know by experience that *true religion* is a union of the soul with God, a real participation of the divine nature, the very image of God drawn upon the soul, or, in the apostle's phrase, it is Christ formed within us.

—Henry Scougal
(1650-1678)
The Life of God in the Soul of Man
Professor of Theology; Bishop of Aberdeen

SHALL SUCH BE FOUND WISE

Labour for the experience of religion in your own souls, that you may have an argument for the reality of it from your spiritual sense and feeling; and cleave to the Lord in His way of holiness (without which you shall not see the Lord), His work also, His interests, and people in all hazards, being assured that such shall be found wise in the end.

—Thomas Boston of Ettrick
(1676-1732)
Diary

(For benefit of his children)

WE KNOW NOT...WE SEE NOT

He who is the revealer of God to man is also the revealer of man to himself. Apart from Christ we know not our God, and apart from Christ we know not ourselves: as, indeed, it is also true, that we are as slow to apprehend and to welcome the one revelation as the other—as slow to see man in Christ, as to see God in Christ.

—John McLeod Campbell
(1800-1872)
The Nature of the Atonement

Minister, Rhu

NATURE IS ROOTED IN GRACE

Men have often crucified the Spirit of Truth, but from its lips they shall never hear the words, "It is finished." For along with the realisation that the world in which we find ourselves is ultimately a spiritual world, goes the sense that Nature is actually rooted and only fulfilled in grace, because it is a world into which in the fulness of the times One came Who not only was the revelation of the heart of God but Who is now, as He was in the days of His flesh, the only Saviour of mankind.

—James Young Simpson
(1873-1934)
The Attainment of Immortality

Professor of Natural Science, Edinburgh

THE GOD OF WONDERS

O wonderful and inexpressible free, free grace. O wonderful preventing love! Now I see that He is a God that doth wonders; and that all His works are wonders; for He is *Wonderful*. Let then all the angels wonder over this wonderful Wonder; and O my soul, behold it, and wonder also, and long to be there where ye shall have more will and capacity to wonder, and chant and sing over your wonders as new. I shall say no more.

—Sir Robert Hamilton
(1650-1701)
The Christian's Conduct

Laird of Preston

BUT NOW HE IS COME!

The whole gates of my soul lifted up their heads, and the everlasting doors were set open, and the king of glory came in. O stupendous miracle of grace! O astonishing and unexpected visit! But O, when He came near me in the glory of His pardoning grace and mercy, proclaiming Himself the Lord, the Lord God merciful and gracious, long-suffering, etc. How was my soul overwhelmed with His grace! My soul failed when He spoke. But was it any wonder that I was glad? It was rather a wonder that I did not give up the ghost with joy. Was it any wonder though I was glad to see Him whom I had not seen these few years.... But when my Redeemer was absent, O how was His love despised, His name reproached! His spirit vexed by my ungodly deeds. But now He is come! Blessed be His name, who hath taken away the difference.

—Dugald Buchanan
(1716-1768)
Diary

Schoolmaster and Evangelist

TOMORROW ... DO NOT ...

This is Christmas Eve; and tomorrow the Christian world will awake to the gladness of the festival which commemorates the birth of Christ, and men will rejoice and give thanks to God; but do not forget that that which makes our Master's life sacred and memorable to us is not the cradle at Bethlehem but the Cross at Calvary. Do not let any glare or the world's light blind your eyes to the shadow which the Cross casts all along our path. Do not let other voices so fill your ears that you shall give no heed to that one, which says in a tone ever low and clear, "Whosoever does not bear his cross, and come after me, cannot be My disciple."

—Robert Hubert Story
(1835-1907)
Religion and Revelation
Minister, Rosneath; Principal, Glasgow University

TOO SELDOM AT THE CRADLE

We make far too little of the Incarnation; the Fathers knew much more of the incarnate God. Some of them were oftener at Bethlehem than at Calvary; they had too little of Calvary, but they knew Bethlehem well. They took up the Holy Babe in their arms; they loved Immanuel, God with us. We are not too often at the cross, but we are too seldom at the cradle; and we know too little of the Word made flesh, of the Holy Child Jesus.

—John Duncan
(1796-1870)
Recollections
Professor of Hebrew, Edinburgh

WITHOUT HIM ... UNKNOWN

I have ranged about the universe for a proof of God, so far as I could range it, as other people have done; but I have returned like most, empty-handed of everything but this, that He, with whose name we are named, came out from the invisible to this little earth of ours, on purpose to manifest the Father, who is not seen, and without Him is unknown.

—John Bruce
(1794-1880)
Sermon
Minister, St. Andrews, Edinburgh

CHILD WHO INHERITS

Child in the manger,
  Infant of Mary,
Outcast and stranger,
  Lord of all!
Child who inherits
  All our transgressions,
All our demerits
  On Him fall.

—Mary McDonald
(1817-1890)
Translated from Gaelic

WITHIN REACH ... AND LOSE HIM

To be in the midst of the Christian years and not yet to know Him who gives them meaning: to miss Christ though He is passing by in our midst; not to have the sharp, sweet sting of Christmas joy that unto us a child is born, Jesus who saves His people from their sins; to be within reach of His glorious personality and to lose Him, is to lose one's chance of life. No other gain can compensate for missing this. To love Him is to enter into life. To be in Him is to live for evermore. To miss Him, the altogether lovely, is to wrong your own soul. To hate Him is to love death.

—Hugh Black
(1868-1953)
Edinburgh Sermons
Professor, Union Theological Seminary, New York

MAKE THEM YOUR OWN

I daresay in your confinement you will often recur to the first psalm which you ever learned—the twenty-third. It is a beautiful production.... Those who have for their shepherd the living God, shall not, cannot want.... They shall not want nourishment.... They shall not want support.... They shall not want direction.... They shall not want protection.... They shall not want provision.... And they shall not want a future eternal home. Now, my dear Mrs. Steel, just you go over the different parts of this delightful psalm; and as the old divines expressed it, act faith upon them, and make them your own.

> —David Smith
> (1792-1867)
> *Letter: December 22, 1856*

Minister, Biggar

THESE ... ARE THE LAST WORDS

These, O my sons, are the last words I will address to you — that you be at peace and have unfeigned charity among yourselves. If you thus follow the example of the Holy Fathers, God, the Comforter of the good, will be your helper. And I, abiding with Him, will intercede for you. He will not only give you sufficient to supply the wants of this present life, but will also bestow on you the good and eternal rewards which are laid up for those who keep His commandments.

> —St. Columba
> (521-597)
> *His final message to be delivered
> to the Monks by Diarmit*

PRAISE, LAUD, AND BLESS

O, enter then His gates with praise,
Approach with joy His courts unto;
Praise, laud, and bless His name always,
For it is seemly so to do.

For why? the Lord our God is good;
His mercy is for ever sure;
His truth at all times firmly stood,
And shall from age to age endure.

—William Kethe
(1510-1594)
Minister to "English Exiles in Geneva"

INDEX TO CONTRIBUTORS